D0754464

*Ken Uston on Blackjack*

BOOKS BY KEN USTON

*One Third of a Shoe*
*You Can Win at Blackjack in Atlantic City and Las Vegas*
*The Big Player*
*Million Dollar Blackjack*
*Mastering PAC-MAN*
*Score! Beating the Top Sixteen Video Games*
*Ken Uston's Illustrated Guide to Today's Most Popular Computers*
*Ken Uston's Illustrated Guide to Adam*
*Ken Uston's Illustrated Guide to the Apple IIe*
*Ken Uston's Illustrated Guide to the Commodore 64*
*Ken Uston's Illustrated Guide to the Compaq*
*Ken Uston's Illustrated Guide to the IBM PC*
*Ken Uston's Illustrated Guide to the IBM PCjr*
*Ken Uston's Illustrated Guide to the Kaypro*
*Ken Uston's Illustrated Guide to the Macintosh*

# KEN USTON

# *On Blackjack*

**by Ken Uston**

**Lyle Stuart Inc.** **Secaucus, New Jersey**

Published by Lyle Stuart, Inc.
120 Enterprise Ave., Secaucus, N.J. 07094
Published simultaneously in Canada by
Musson Book Company,
A division of General Publishing Co. Limited
Don Mills, Ontario

Address queries regarding rights and permissions to Lyle Stuart, Inc., 120 Enterprise Ave., Secaucus, N.J. 07094

Manufactured in the United States of America

This book is nonfiction, but certain identities, descriptions and facts have been changed to protect the privacy of individuals.

Library of Congress Cataloging-in-Publication Data

Uston, Ken, 1935-
Ken Uston on blackjack.

1. Blackjack (Game) 2. Uston, Ken, 1935-
3. Gamblers—United States—Biography. I. Title.
II. Title: On blackjack.
GV1295.B55U857 1986 795.4'2 [B] 86-14355
ISBN 0-8184-0411-6

TO SENZO USUI
1905—1984

TO ERROLL GARNER
1921—1977

# Publisher's Introduction

Ken Uston is considered by the experts to be the world's foremost blackjack player. Uston and his teams have won more than $5 million in blackjack in casinos in Nevada, Atlantic City, Europe and around the world.

Ken Uston has appeared on national television shows such as "60 Minutes," "Good Morning, America," "The Today Show," "The Merv Griffin Show," "The Mike Douglas Show," "What's My Line," "The Tom Snyder Show," and "To Tell the Truth."

Feature articles about his exploits have appeared in *The New York Times Magazine* (where he rated the cover story) as well as *Time, Newsweek, Sports Illustrated, People, Money, US*, and many other periodicals.

Ken has written 17 books, including four on blackjack. His first, *The Big Player* (Holt, Rinehart & Winston, 1977), is being made into a major motion picture by Dale Crase–Frank Capra Jr. Productions.

His previous book on blackjack (*Million Dollar Blackjack*), written more than five years ago, has been widely acclaimed as the most complete book ever written on the game of blackjack. It was listed for weeks on the *Philadelphia Inquirer* best-seller list.

After that, Ken Uston became fascinated with the world of video games and home computers, and wrote 11 books on those subjects, including *Mastering PAC-MAN* (three million copies in print), which appeared on *The New York Times* best-seller list for several weeks. He also authored three other books on video games, and seven books on home computers.

In February, 1984, a chance encounter led Ken Uston to return to the world of blackjack. He took a skiing trip to Lake Tahoe. Playing some après ski blackjack, he was soon recognized in Caesars Palace, where he was prevented from playing.

Ken documented the circumstances surrounding this barring and went on to play at three other major Lake Tahoe casinos. Eventually, after winning several thousand dollars, he was barred at those casinos as well.

When he returned to the Bay Area, Ken wrote up the Tahoe episodes and sent off a letter of complaint to the Nevada Gaming Commission. This started a chain of legal events, leading to appeals to the Nevada court system.

While in Las Vegas pursuing his legal right to play blackjack, Ken scouted out the various casinos and discovered that the games were highly beatable.

He formed a team. During his dozens of hours of practice preparing for play, he discovered that many of the techniques he had previously used—indeed the very system that he had designed—had become obsolete.

When the team started playing, Ken found that the game had become much tougher, primarily because pit bosses had become familiar with the techniques of card-counting. Pit bosses who hadn't seen Ken in years recognized and barred him, even though he was in disguise. The initial team foundered for several months and finally disbanded.

Developing new techniques to cope with the more difficult environment, Uston formed a second group, and launched his assault on the casinos once again.

The book you hold in your hands is the story of that tumultuous period in Ken Uston's life. It relates the winning and losing of tens of thousands of dollars, the cloak-and-dagger, cops-and-robbers experiences of professional blackjack teams, the battle with the Nevada Gaming Commission, the casinos, and the Nevada Attorney General in the courts, and the new techniques Ken Uston developed to beat the casinos at their own very profitable game.

# Acknowledgments

This book was made possible because of the work of the outstanding contributors to the game of blackjack—the theoreticians, the practitioners, and the legal experts.

I'm indebted to four men who, when the dust settles, will be known as the greatest contributors to the world's knowledge of the game of blackjack:

—Dr. Ed Thorp
—"Lawrence Revere"
—"Stanford Wong"
—"Arnold Snyder"

Dr. Thorp, of course, started it all with his classic text, *Beat the Dealer,* first published in 1961. The late "Lawrence Revere" (whose real name was Spec Parsons), although not the practitioner many thought he was, developed several simple but powerful counting systems in the early 1970's.

"Stanford Wong" has made many contributions with his mathematical analyses and computer simulations of the game. Finally, "Arnold Snyder" is one of the few blackjack experts who's managed to stay above the competitive fray, while maintaining a keen sense of humor. Arnold advanced our knowledge of blackjack in many areas, particularly with regard to the comparison of counting systems, winning rates, and statistical fluctuations.

—Mel Horowitz
—"Junior"
—Bill Erb

Mel Horowitz, who died in 1985, was one of the very first players to use a count system, starting in the 1950's. (Mel helped me finance the legal effort in New Jersey and introduced me to the legal experts who masterminded that project.) "Junior," one of the youngest early players, counted and used shuffle-tracking far before the computers showed that these techniques were viable.

Bill Erb, a former teammate, a superb player, and a close friend, is one of the few players who can claim to have played over a million hands of winning blackjack.

Two magnificent legal minds helped the cause:

—Morris Goldings
—Les Combs

Morris Goldings' creativity and tenacity led to the historic 1982 New Jersey Supreme Court decision forbidding Atlantic City casinos from preventing me, and other skillful players, from playing blackjack.

Les Combs, a former blackjack teammate and now a Las Vegas lawyer, continues to protect the rights of barred card-counters in Nevada.

# Foreword

It's a privilege to introduce Ken's book. As a player for 15 years—and a member of three of Ken's teams—I can tell you that the inside knowledge and creative techniques included in this volume are priceless.

This book contains a unique blend of theoretical knowledge and playing experience. It could have been written only by Ken.

One thing should be cleared up, however. In the acknowledgments section, Ken's name, without doubt, belongs on all three lists.

—BILL ERB

# Contents

# 1

# Blackjack, *60 Minutes*, PAC-MAN, and Home Computers

It's been a long time since I got that telephone call back in 1974 that changed my life—and dozens of other lives as well.

I was sitting in my office in the San Francisco financial district. The call came in from a fellow whom I'll call Al Francesco. The conversation went something like this:

"I unnerstan' you know something about blackjack."

I responded, "Yeah, I've studied it."

"Well, I gotta team of players, we're up about 60 grand. We play in Vegas, and I'm lookin' for more players."

Al told me a little more about his team and the system he used (a quite complicated one, called the Revere 14 Count). I became intrigued, and the very next day I drove over to Al's house in the East Bay.

Al was short, swarthy, and spoke with a Brooklyn accent. Before long, he convinced me that he knew a great deal about blackjack and had been successful at it. Five players were sitting around a blackjack table in his living room, practicing.

Well, that visit eventually led me to put my Brooks Brothers three-piece suits in moth-balls, leave my job as Senior Vice President of the Pacific Stock Exchange, and embark on a career as a professional blackjack player.

Over the next six years, Al's team, and the five teams I organized, won well into seven figures playing blackjack. We played in Las Vegas, Reno, Tahoe, France, England, the Orient—virtually everyplace where there was a beatable blackjack game. Nearly all our team members had their lives changed—most, I believe, for the better.

But becoming proficient at blackjack is different from becoming a star baseball player or moving up the hierarchy in a corporation. When you get good, you don't get promoted or advance your career. Instead, you get "fired," because the casinos in most countries retain the right to forbid skillful blackjack players from playing. By 1978, pit bosses on every shift in every casino in Vegas, Reno and Lake Tahoe knew me by sight, despite my numerous disguises over the years. In short, I couldn't pursue my chosen profession in Nevada.

During that same year, casinos opened up in Atlantic City. My career was extended temporarily.

I formed a team of six players and brought them to Atlantic City in January, 1979. We played at Resorts International, the only game in town at that time.

In about three weeks, we won $145,000. Then, for the first time in New Jersey history, our team and other card-counters were thrown out, prevented from playing by order of the Gaming Commission. Resorts put up signs that proclaimed:

PROFESSIONAL BLACKJACK PLAYERS ARE PROHIBITED FROM PLAY AT OUR BLACKJACK TABLES.

It would take me nearly four years to get those signs taken down.

During the following summer, I bankrolled several teammates, who beat Resorts for about $300,000.

Eleven months later, in December, 1979, the New Jersey Casino Control Commission tried an experiment. Blackjack counters once again were allowed to play in Atlantic City, but under restricted playing conditions.

The experiment lasted 14 days, and then Commission Chairman Joseph Lordi called it off. Our nine-member team won $350,000—from Resorts and Caesars Palace, the two casinos that were then open in Atlantic City.

Our team had nearly $500,000 in cash (we'd started with $100,000) in flimsy safe deposit offices in the two casinos. To say I was nervous about getting ripped off was an understatement.

When we used to work with still-respectable sums of $40,000 or $50,000, we used to say, "They rob banks for a lot less."

In this case, one teammate said, "They have revolutions in countries for what we've got in those boxes."

I hired two off-duty Atlantic City cops to serve as bodyguards, when we opened the boxes before and after each session. But that led to yet another worry: Would the cops double-cross us and set us up for a "hit" by their accomplices?

As it turned out, our team managed to get the nearly half-million out of Atlantic City without incident.

When that "trip," as we call them, was over, I took a long vacation. I went to Newport Beach and for five months did absolutely nothing other than run on the beach, party and relax, or, as they said in those days, enjoy "sex, drugs, and rock and roll." Of course, that didn't apply to me—I like jazz.

## *60 Minutes* Gets into the Act

In May, I got a call from producer Drew Phillips of the TV show *60 Minutes*. He'd heard about my pending court case against the Atlantic City casinos for the right to play blackjack. *60 Minutes* was interested in doing a story about the controversy.

Drew flew out to our bachelor pad in Newport Beach the following week, met with some of my teammates, and interviewed me. The next day, he and I flew to Vegas.

With Drew standing behind me, I tried to play at the Aladdin, the Mint, Sahara, the Dunes. Everywhere we went, we ran into the same concrete wall:

"Sorry, Kenny, we don't want your action.

"Kenny, why don't you and your friend have dinner in our gourmet room," basically a bribe to get me to stop playing blackjack.

In several places, the pit bosses just brusquely pushed my bet back and told the dealer to deal around me.

Drew was flabbergasted at this treatment. He thought it totally unfair. He flew back to New York. In less than two weeks he returned to Las Vegas with a film crew. He wired me for sound, and the cameraman followed me around the casinos, with a hidden camera, ready to record my next barring.

I had no trouble getting barred. The trouble was that the cameraman, a likeable Philadelphian named Walt, had hidden his camera in a shoulder-mounted airlines bag, which made it difficult to aim. Walt had to shoot "from the vest."

Walt's nervousness made the situation worse. He'd read too much fiction about Vegas and the Mafia connection and was deathly afraid of being found dead in the desert for violating the posted rule prohibiting photography in casinos.

After each day's shooting, Drew flew the film to photo labs in Los Angeles for developing.

Invariably the word from the film lab the next day was, "You got terrific pictures of the ceiling and floors, but none of Ken."

So it was off to another casino, again wired for sound, to get barred once again for the benefit of the cameras.

Finally, after two weeks, the preliminary "shoot" was over. Now it was time for Harry Reasoner to come into town to ask the casino bosses how they justified throwing me out.

Harry, a gentle soul, didn't feel comfortable in this role. On several occasions, he readily admitted, "I wish they'd gotten Mike [Wallace] for this job."

Our entourage headed for the Holiday Riverboat; there was Harry, Harry's girlfriend, me and my girlfriend, Drew, the cameraman, and several other technicians.

As Harry and I approached one of the bosses, a technician aimed bright lights into the pit. Harry said:

"Hi. I'm Harry Reasoner. This is Ken Uston. I understand he's not allowed to play in your casino."

The boss hemmed and hawed. Harry asked a series of questions:

"Why can't Ken play in your casino?"

"Do you bar players for being too good?"

"If Ken is an orderly man, why can't he play blackjack here?"

The boss ducked each one of the questions and came across looking real silly.

Then our group went to the Flamingo Hilton. We got a hilarious shot of a portly pit boss waving his arms wildly and screaming, "Turn out those lights!" That turned out to be the closing shot of the edited segment.

Millions of Americans saw those episodes on their television screens. The piece was aired twice. It made the casinos' position look absurd. I'm convinced that *60 Minutes* was enormously helpful in a later legal battle with the Atlantic City casinos.

## The $24,000 *60 Minutes* Aftermath

The Las Vegas newspapers publicized the fact that Harry Reasoner and the *60 Minutes* crew were in town filming me being barred from casinos. When the crew left town, we used this publicity to good advantage.

I strolled into the Mint with a young ladyfriend. We were spotted the minute we walked in the door. Despite this, I walked up to a table and threw $1,000 on the table. I stage-whispered to my companion:

"Hope he's got it focused," looking over at the crowded bar, as if someone was there with a hidden camera.

The ploy worked. They allowed me to play.

After a half hour, up $3,400, I gathered in the chips, and threw a black one ($100) to the dealer.

The boss came over,

"Are you through now, Kenny?"

I had to laugh. A few weeks earlier, it would have been, "Get your ass out of here."

"Yes, I am. Thank you very much."

The Mint, a hard-nosed club that photographed and back-roomed suspected card-counters, had let me play because they believed *60 Minutes* was filming the play!

For the next three days I repeated this subterfuge at the Sands, the Dunes, MGM, Ceasars and the Hilton.

Twenty-four thousand dollars later, it was time to go to Newport Beach again—to recreate.

## My Libido Leads to a *New York Times* Best-Seller

It's nice living in Atlantic City—about four months of the year. It was 1981 and for the third summer in a row I found myself in the oceanside town, walking the "boards," playing jazz piano in local clubs, and just basically hanging out. I had some legal work to do as well—to force the casinos to allow me to play.

The Playboy casino had just opened. Hefner and company had flown in a bevy of bunnies from Chicago and New York to help train local girls to be bunnies.

The Playboy Club was at the corner of Florida Avenue and the Boardwalk. Right down the street is a bar called Easy Street, where the bunnies hung out after work. I had never before seen such a collection of puchritude in my life. For obvious reasons, I, too, hung out there.

By chance, Easy Street had two PAC-MAN machines. I played the game for hours on end.

PAC-MAN's a lot like blackjack (mathematicians would say, "Both are deterministic"):

—In blackjack, the dealer must play the hand exactly in accordance with the rules, hitting until the house total is 17 or greater.

—In PAC-MAN, the little monsters are programmed to react in a pre-determined way, in response to the way the player moves his smiling yellow disk around the board.

After about 50 hours playing the game, I started to become familiar with how the machine was programmed. I drew charts and schematics of the various "boards" until, after another 200 hours or so, I had developed patterns which, when followed, would allow the player to win so steadily that he could play one game indefinitely.

An Easy Street waitress suggested I write a book about PAC-MAN. I followed her suggestion and then contacted a New York literary agent. Then I went to Manila with a team to play some blackjack (to this day, Philippine rules are among the best in the world).

Three days later, the agent called the Manila hotel to tell me that New American Library (NAL) wanted to publish the PAC-MAN book, and had offered an advance of $25,000.

When the trip ended (our team broke even after ten days of frustrating play), I flew to New York to sign the contract. A snag developed. Bally, who manufactured PAC-MAN, heard about the forthcoming book and called NAL, asking for a copy of the manuscript. Hoping they'd endorse the book, we sent them the manuscript immediately.

Two days later, my agent called.

"Ken, the president of Bally read your book. He said 'The book is too good—we can't allow it to be published—people'll be playing forever on one quarter.' Bally's going to sue if the book is published."

Now consider the irony of this. I'd been thrown out of New Jersey casinos for playing blackjack too well. One of the casinos was Bally's Park Place.

This same company was now telling me I couldn't publish a book about a video game because it would help the customers play too well. I saw red (a few months later, I got to vent my spleen about this absurdity on national TV—while playing PAC-MAN with Jane Pauley on the *Today* show. That show got NAL worrying about a libel suit, to boot).

NAL, God bless 'em, went ahead. They turned their offices upside down to get that book out. In publishing, it usually takes six to nine months or more to publish a book. If a book is "crashed," it takes perhaps three months.

I submitted the manuscript to NAL on the 1st of February. On February 21, NAL shipped a half a million copies across the country. The following week the book was on *The New York Times* and *Publishers Weekly* best-seller lists. (Three million copies were eventually printed.)

Because of the video-game mania sweeping the country, NAL asked me to do a book on beating the top dozen arcade games (400,000 copies). Then an 800-page tome on playing the 180 home video games then in existence (250,000 copies). And an update on the newer video games, which were coming out in droves. And a book on home computers, the newest American obsession.

Then Prentice-Hall called. They wanted me to do a series of books on home computers—seven in all. So the years 1981 and 1982 were spent frenetically writing a dozen books.

I took a year off, traveling to the Orient, the Caribbean, and elsewhere. It was during this year that I also took the trip to Lake Tahoe which was to bring me full-circle, back into blackjack once again.

# 2

# A Chance Tahoe Skiing Vacation Starts It All Over Again

The month was February, 1984. My fiancée, Inga, and I were off to Tahoe—to ski, party, see Joan Rivers, and enjoy some chateaubriand and Dom Perignon.

I also brought along ten thousand dollars, just in case.

We drove our rented Hertz-mobile up scenic Route 50 and checked in to Harrah's, my favorite Northern Nevada Hotel—where else does one get two johns in every room, each with a miniature TV, and a personal 24-hour computer-controlled wetbar, with cocktails and hors d'oeuvres, to say nothing of a phenomenal continental penthouse restaurant overlooking the lake, and the natural beauty of wood-glass-stone architecture?

After a day of mogul-hopping, we were killing some time in Harrah's huge casino. The juicy single deck games were too good to resist (most dealers were dealing three-quarters of the deck, a good sign for the card-counter—the more cards seen, the better the probability of winning).

I spotted an empty $25 table. My first glance, as always, was to the pit, to check out the bosses. Nothing but youngish-looking Yuppie floormen. Not a single familiar face.

Time for some après ski blackjack. I threw $500 on the table, saying, "Red and black," meaning, "Give me $5 and $25 chips" (most casinos use green $25 chips; Harrah's uses black).

After a few rounds, the deck went good.* I ran out of chips. I bet a $100 bill (the bosses like it when you run out of money and play cash—"The loser's steaming"). I lost again. The count went even higher (the cards favored the player by about 5%), I bet $300. Another loss.

By now, the boss was salivating. He came over and gave me his card:

"Anything you want, let me know".

I played for about an hour, varying from $25 to $300.** It looked as if I'd found a place to play this trip—that was the good news. The bad—I was down five grand.

Time for dinner.

The boss called up, and Inga and I went to their Summit rooftop restaurant. We ordered it up as much as possible, figuring we'd gastronomically recoup some of the five grand on our "comp."

Why is it, whenever we get a "comp," the wine list seems to be limited? The top wine we could find was a Chateauneuf-du-Pape, at $45 per. (Of course, when we're paying, the wine list is replete with Dom Perignons and Lafite Rothschilds). So naturally we ordered two bottles and Cherries Jubilee for dessert. Despite our best efforts, we managed only to eat up about $200 worth.

Back to the casino. Within ten minutes, I recouped $2,000. But there was a serious cloud on the horizon: I spotted a face in the pit that looked familiar.

I was right. Within minutes, my "friendly" boss came over.

*Counters keep track of the types of cards that are played. When the "count goes up" or "the deck gets good," the odds have become favorable to the player.

**Counters make bigger bets when the deck favors the player, and small bets when the bets favor the house. Generally, the larger the variation in bet size, the higher the advantage enjoyed by the counter.

"Sorry, Kenny, we can't let you play blackjack anymore."

"But I'm down three grand."

The boss shook his head apologetically.

I said, "Tell you what. The hell with the three grand. I'm going to be here four days, skiing. How about comping my room? I promise I won't play here the entire trip."

The boss disappeared. Five minutes later came back and said, "OK. But remember, no playing."

"You got a deal."

It turned out we were RFB'd (complimentary Room, Food and Beverage).

The next morning, the phone rang.

"Ken, this is Bill Jones, I'm in charge of 21 at Harrah's."

I thought, "Uh, oh. Now what?"

Bill went on, "I wonder if I could buy you breakfast."

The offer was academic since we were RFB, but I agreed to meet him in the coffee shop.

I'd never seen Bill before. He was young, bright, reasonably articulate, cordial and friendly. He knew a few things about card-counting and basically just wanted to meet me and talk some blackjack.

When it came to spotting counters, he said (typical of all bosses who think they know it all), "Oh, I always catch them. I just look for bet variation."

I asked, "What kind of a ratio you look for?"

"If I see a four-to-one, I watch closely. Believe me, we spot counters real quick."

I said, "Bill, I'll bet you I'll put down a 50-to-1 ratio, and you wouldn't pick up on it."

He looked highly skeptical. I continued, "If you want, let's go to one of the other casinos, and I'll show how it's done."

He accepted, inviting us to his home that night for dinner before the little exhibition.

Bill lived high in the Tahoe hills, so high I could hardly get my breath because of the thinness of the air. After a sumptuous meal, prepared by Bill's fiancée, a blackjack dealer, we drove to the Nugget casino, one of the smaller joints at the Lake.

We went up to a table and I cashed in for $200 in chips. I ordered a drink, saying, "Make it a double," real loud so the pit boss heard.

Flat betting* a green ($25) chip for a while to get them used to that level, I pushed the bet up to $50. Lost. The count went down.

Out with a nickel chip. No heat** yet.

The count went up. I threw out $100. The dealer shuffled.

I added four more chips to the next betting square, making two bets of $100, off-the-top.*** (What I was trying to convey was: "I'm not watching the cards—I'm a hunch better. I think I'm going to win the next round. I wasn't aware of your shuffling—what's the difference, anyway?")

The next time the dealer shuffled, I went $100 off-the-top (same message).

The boss who had been watching the game shrugged and walked away.

Now the place was mine. Five dollars, $25, $100, two hands of $100. To be a little dramatic for Bill's benefit, I bet $2 when the deck went really bad. If I lost, and the count went up, I'd impetuously throw out $100.

To pour it on, we also ordered four rounds of drinks.

No heat. The bosses were salivating, ready to fleece this carefree, drunken high-roller.

Bill scratched his head and whispered to me,

"I don't believe this."

We won about $600, no small amount for a tiny club like the Nugget. I picked up the chips and we headed for the bar. The boss signalled the bartender to serve us, on-the-house.

It was an upbeat moment. (Of course, it could have gone the other way, because any time I play for a half hour or so, the chances of winning are just slightly over 50%.)

*"Flat betting" is betting the same amount every hand. It is usually impossible for the counter to win money at blackjack by flat betting.

**"Heat" is a term often employed by card-counters to designate that a casino employee, usually a pit boss, has detected their method of play. Heat is often followed by the pit boss's barring a counter, or sometimes taking even more extreme action, including arrest and, in rare cases, physical abuse.

***An off-the-top bet is a bet made immediately after the deck or cards are shuffled. Since the counter must almost always first see some cards before knowing he has the edge, the counter does not usually have an edge when he makes an off-the-top bet.

A counter may make large off-the-top bets as "cover"—that is, to delude casino employees into thinking that he is not a skillful player.

We drove to Harvey's Inn. I spotted a dealer going real deep in the deck.* The limit here was $200 per hand. I decided to up the stakes a little.

All four of us were in a festive, partying mood. We were loud, laughing, and a bit raucous. I was acting real drunk, intentionally slurring my words. I cashed in for $1,000 and made an opening bet of $25.

"Just testin' the water."

The boss watching the game was a friendly, smiling woman, Jeannie Stead. She seemed quite amused with our partying. Every once in a while, though, I thought I detected a questioning look, as if she suspected I might be me. (I'd made absolutely no effort to disguise myself.)

The deck went positive.** Time to start moving the bets up. I "drunkenly" threw out $100. The dealer didn't shuffle. Time to order another round for the four of us. (Translation: "Booze loosens me up—the more I drink, the higher I bet.")

Now it was time to really go nuts. I spread to three hands—a nickel ($5 chip) on the first, a quarter on the second, and a nickel on the third. Just before the dealer started throwing out the cards, I yelled:

"Stop!"

I "superstitiously" reversed the quarter and the nickel bets, yelling, "No, no, that's the lucky spot—there!" Yes, I was getting a bit obnoxious. But that was fine.

It's OK if they think you're obnoxious—as long as they don't think you're smart.

The dealer was going way down in the deck. Now I was the only player at the table, so I didn't have to worry about being caught looking at any other players' cards. All the cards were mine.

Jeannie still looked skeptical. To get her securely in our corner, I'd periodically walk away from the table, after I played my hands. I'd

*Since the counter capitalizes on knowing what types of cards have been played, he usually has a greater edge when the dealer deals further, or deeper, into the deck(s).

**The counter assigns + (plus) values to cards that benefit him, when played. He assigns − (minus) values to cards that benefit the house, when played. Thus the deck is plus, or positive, when the odds favor the counter (also referred to as "the count is high"). The odds tend to favor the house when the deck is negative (i.e., "the count is low").

cover my eyes with my hands, saying, "I don't want to sweat it out—just tell me whether I won or lost."

I'd return to the table after the dealer played her hand, settled the bets, and collected the cards. This way, I had hoped, Jeannie would think, "This guy **is** some nut—certainly no card-counter—he doesn't even look at the dealer's hole card and the cards she drew."

This technique, by the way, is a profitable subterfuge. You periodically miss seeing one or two cards—a minor sacrifice compared with the opportunity of getting huge betting spreads and cards dealt further into the deck, the two most important factors which determine the edge enjoyed by the card-counter. This technique has worked for me in dozens and dozens of clubs.

Now it was time for a $200 bet. The first one was off-the-top, for cover purposes. I won the hand; the deck went up. I screamed loudly, like they do at the craps table, and said, "OK. This is it! How many hands of $200 can I bet?"

Jeannie said, "Up to three."

I said, "OK," and shoved out three bets of $200.

Jeannie smiled. What card-counter would loudly proclaim a tripling of bet size? I boisterously ordered another round of drinks (we'd hardly touched the previous one), saying, "Make mine a double."

I won and played three more hands of $200. Won again. Shuffle. One hand of $40, one hand of $50 and a final hand of one quarter, six reds, seven silver ($1), and two half dollars—actually a huge stack, but worth only $63. Thus the bet was cut way down for the opening round, but it looked like there was a ton of money at stake.

Lose two hands, win one. The deck goes down. I say, "No way. The cards are turning," and, once again, for Bill's benefit, I break it off by putting out a $2 bet.

Finally, after going ahead about $2,500, I asked Jeannie for a rack. I filled it up with chips and threw a quarter chip to the dealer. Jeannie asked if we wanted dinner and comped us at the restaurant.

In the restaurant, I asked Bill, "If you had seen this at Harrah's, would you have pulled the play up?"

Bill said, "No, in all honesty, I wouldn't have. It didn't look like a counting play."

We ordered. Before our food was served, a tall, fat security guard suddenly came up to our table. In a decidedly unfriendly tone, he growled, "You can't play here no more."

I said, "Yessir."

Despite my acquiescence, he repeated his unwelcome remark a couple of times.

We left the restaurant, I cashed out, and it was out the door of Harvey's Inn.

## Neil Lewis Becomes the Answer to a Trivia Question

The following night, a totally unexpected incident led to the Nevada lawsuit.

Inga and I went with some friends to Caesars to play a few hands, just for fun.

I taught one friend some hand signals—for how much to bet and to hit, stand, double or split. The friend, Steve, was coincidentally a fellow I had practiced blackjack with ten years before when we both worked for Cresap, McCormick and Paget, a straight-laced management consulting firm.

We went to a table. I bet only $5 per hand, but signaled Steve so he could vary from $25 to $100. Steve, who'd obviously had a few drinks, didn't look at the other players' cards. Thus the pit wouldn't suspect Steve of card-counting. Steve and I pretended we didn't know each other.

Things were going fine. Yet one boss seemed to be looking at me too often. I sensed that he may have recognized me, but since I was only flat-betting nickels, he couldn't have cared less.

Then Steve misread a signal and split tens against a ten—a horrible play. I turned to him and said:

"You don't want to do that."

The boss, overhearing, said to me:

"Let him play his own hand."

On the very next round, the boss stage whispered to the dealer, "Deal around him," nodding in my direction.

Not getting any cards, I turned to the boss and asked, "What's going on?"

He ignored me.

Louder this time, I said, “Why didn’t I get my cards?”

The boss, giving me a real dirty look, said, “I don’t want your action.”

I asked, “Why not?”

Once again the boss ignored me.

I saw red and blurted, “OK, Buddy. Because of you, I’m going to start a lawsuit out here, too. What’s your name?”

“Neil Lewis.”

I asked for the shift manager. A guy named Joe Beachboard came over. He, too, said that I couldn’t play, but at least he was friendly.

“Kenny, why not have a few drinks on me?”

We adjourned to the nearby Spooner Lounge. I kept Joe’s comp slip, just in case I’d have to establish that the barring was not due to any misbehavior on my part, but solely because of card-counting.

Over the next several days, I was barred at Harvey’s and the High Sierra. In both cases, I kept careful records of the date, time, table number, and the dealer’s name, and got business cards from the pit bosses. I also made sure I had witnesses.

The battle had begun.

# 3

# After Ten Years, Another Try for a Commission Hearing

I had all the evidence I needed to start legal proceedings—good solid proof of being barred from four casinos for no reason other than being skillful at blackjack.

I wasn't sure if I wanted to proceed. Sure, we'd won a similar case in New Jersey a couple of years ago. But that effort cost more than $100,000 in legal fees and took enormous amounts of my time.

Further, Nevada isn't New Jersey. When we won in New Jersey, the casino industry was a fledgling onc, just a tiny portion of the New Jersey economy.

In Nevada, the gaming industry was, and still is, the lion who controls the jungle. It's been said that some 60% of the meals put on the tables in Nevada stem directly or indirectly from the casino industry. This includes the thousands of employees, suppliers, restaurants, motels, and other cottage industries that exist because of the legalized gaming.

And poor legal precedents had been established in Nevada. A full ten years ago, I sued several casinos for the right to play. Because our efforts were disorganized, we went head-on against the "Good ol' boy" network in Nevada and fell flat on our faces.

What chance would we have of getting an objective hearing now? I'd get discouraged when people reminded me that "A judge is nothing but a lawyer with political connections." After all, even Ronald Reagan's buddy, ex-Senator Laxalt, had had an interest in the Ormsby Hotel-Casino in Carson City and was involved in a controversy involving skimming.

## The Early Legal Attempt in Nevada

The first blackjack team I was part of was organized by Al Francesco and played in Las Vegas and in Europe. During the years 1973 through 1975, the team won just over $1 million—half of it in Vegas.

I was busted on my last play for this team. I'd been playing from one to five hands of $1,000 for eight straight weeks at the Sands. For a while, they loved the action. I was given hotel suites, bottles of Dom Perignon, ringside seats at shows, and a slew of invitations to celebrity golf tournaments.

Then, one weekend, with $45,000 in the cage, I was expelled from the Sands—after being read the Trespass Act (i.e., if I even walked into the Sands or any other Hughes casino, I'd be subject to arrest).

I took my money and went to the Dunes. In two hours, I was kicked out of there, too (the Sands had called).

I hired a fledgling San Francisco attorney, who, it turned out, was average, at best. This was the first of many times I was to learn that hiring inexpensive legal representation can be a false economy.

We filed suits against both the Sands and the Dunes.

I also had a Nevada lawyer write to the Commission asking for its position on card-counting. The letter, dated May 21, 1976, was never answered. This would be the first of a dozen or so times that the Commission, a public agency, would stonewall on the issue.

Several months later, I made an experimental trip to Vegas. Incredibly, I could still get games all over town. I organized my own team. We won $650,000 in eight months. In the process, I was barred from just about every club in town.

We followed the first two lawsuits with more legal action. To get attention, we asked for a total of $81 million in damages:

| *Casino Sued* | *Amount* |
|---|---|
| The Hilton | $24.0 million |
| Flamingo | 15.0 million |
| Sands | 12.0 million |
| Marina | 12.0 million |
| Silver City | 9.0 million |
| MGM Grand | 8.0 million |
| Dunes | 1.2 million |
| TOTAL | $81.2 million |

We filed first in San Francisco Federal Court, arguing that the casinos had violated basic constitutional rights by barring me from a public place solely for being skillful.

The judge ruled that there was no constitutional right to gamble and threw the cases out.

Then we went to Nevada Federal Court. The paperwork was so poorly prepared that the judge threw out the cases "without prejudice" (i.e., "if you want to, you can try again").

At that time, I was so busy playing blackjack in Europe and the Orient that I didn't seek a new lawyer. Although we settled the Dunes and Sands cases out of court, the other lawsuits died a natural death. They would come back to haunt us years later.

So much for trying to battle the Nevada legal system.

## The Successful Atlantic City Battle

In January, 1979, I put together a team of six players to play at Resorts in Atlantic City. We won $145,000, but were thrown out after two weeks—as were many other counters. I decided to stay in AC to fight the legal battle.

During that time, I ran into a legendary blackjack player, who had made millions from casinos all over the world since the '50s. His name was Mel Horowitz, who was so incensed at Resorts' barring me that he agreed to help finance the lawsuit. We used his attorney, Morris Goldings, a brilliant Boston constitutional lawyer.

I filed the complaint with the New Jersey Gaming Commission. As expected, the Commission ruled for Resorts. We appealed to the New Jersey Appellate Court.

The casinos' legal position depended on the centuries-old English Innkeeper's Act, which gave a business the common law right to exclude anyone they choose (as long as the exclusion did not violate the subsequently adopted civil rights laws).

Our position was that the Innkeeper's Act was superceded (or "abrogated," as the lawyers said) by sections of the Casino Control Act which specify those persons who may be excluded from New Jersey casinos (such as known felons and unsavory persons).

The Appellate Court ruled in our favor—unanimously.

Now it was Resorts' turn to file an appeal—with the New Jersey Supreme Court.

After two years of motions, counter-motions, and a lengthy court hearing (to our surprise, New Jersey's Attorney General appeared in our behalf), the Supreme Court made a landmark decision. They ruled that New Jersey casinos could not bar me or anyone else for being a skillful player.* The ruling was made effective September 15, 1982.

The bottom line was that we won the battle but lost the war. The casinos put in eight-deck games. Worse yet, the Commission permitted the casinos to shuffle cards any time they wanted to. Thus, when a pit boss spotted a counter, he could simply have the cards

*The Court's decision purposely left open the question of whether the Commission, as opposed to the casinos, could bar players. However, the wording of the decision hinted strongly that the Commission would be advised to carefully consider the implications of giving itself that power.

In a later hearing on this issue, I represented counters versus over a dozen casino lawyers, gaming "experts" and others. The casinos wanted the Commission to bar counters so bad they could taste it; they sent experts in to testify that the game would be ruined, threatened that blackjack would no longer be offered by them, and made numerous other absurd allegations.

The Commission ruled in our favor and the casinos didn't discontinue the game.

pulled out of the shoe and shuffled whenever the counter placed a large wager.

## Why I Went to Court

Lots of people ask me why I keep battling the casinos, "because they'll just make the game tougher."

My answer to this is:

"Go out and play yourself, get barred, insulted, jostled into backrooms, and photographed against your will—maybe even punched. You'll change your attitude in a hurry."

Many teammates could never understand my militant position on this issue—until their first barring. Then they, too, became outraged and wanted to sue. It's something you have to experience yourself to understand. I guess it's like being hijacked, mugged, or kidnapped. (As a current bad joke goes, "A conservative is a liberal who's been mugged.")

I had other reasons. A few years back, I was a guest at the Mapes casino in Reno. I was a comped high-roller, with ten thousand in the cage, and was playing in a cowboy disguise ("My name's Billy Williams, but my real friends call me Tex").

On the fourth day of play someone in the pit recognized me and I was thrown out. The security guard, a six-foot-two ex-Coast Guard boxer, apparently missed pugalism, because he popped me in the face when I wasn't looking. (He denies the sucker punch, claiming I took the first swing. I haven't thrown a punch in my adult life.)

I ended up in a hospital with multiple fractures of the cheek bone. As I write this, years later, I still have a tight sensation in my face from that ordeal.

On another occasion, while I was battling Resorts in the courts, a car driven by a New Jersey detective went the wrong way down the one-way entrance to Resorts in Atlantic City. Of the hundreds of thousands of people driving through that entrance, I'll bet he's the only one that ever drove in that direction (if you've ever been to Resorts, you'll know what I mean.)

The car hit me and broke my leg. The police reports, incredibly, read, "Pedestrian walks into moving vehicle."

Do the cops protect each other, or what?

## I Decide to Fight City Hall

When the Tahoe barrings took place, I was in between projects—mostly traveling, watching TV, partying—basically killing time and feeling a little guilty about it. Thinking it was time to do something constructive, I decided to take another crack at the Nevada legal system.

The first question inevitably was what to do about lawyers. No way would I spend another $100,000 to prove a legal point.

At the time, I had a small army of lawyers under retainer:

—A Connecticut lawyer was working to collect royalties owed to me by Coleco for a blackjack video game.

—A California lawyer was trying to collect royalties withheld by *Gambling Times* Magazine.

—Two Ohio lawyers were trying to protect my assets from ex-wife number one.

—A California lawyer was trying to keep me in a rent-controlled San Francisco apartment. (The rent was $700; if the landlord got me out, he'd be able to lease it for $2,300.)

I didn't want to add to this list.

I thought back to the times I'd fought the New Jersey casinos, representing myself—*in pro per*, as it's called.*

The casinos had spent, I was told, over one-half million dollars in legal fees. I hadn't spent a dime. We won.

This experience led me to believe that I might be able to battle Nevada basically on my own, keeping the work done by attorneys down to a bare minimum.

So I would challenge the Nevada casinos *in pro per*. Here's how the opening salvos went:

*March 1, 1984*

I wrote to the Gaming Control Board, requesting a hearing to consider whether casinos could exclude me from playing. In-

*This was an attempt to get the "surrender" player option restored, which it was—but for only six days. The Governor rescinded the option, declaring a state "emergency."

cluded was a notarized affidavit describing the four Tahoe barrings.

*April 2, 1984*

Gaming Control Board Chairman James Avance (more about him later) replied:

"The hearing you request would be more appropriately handled as consideration of a proposed regulation."

Avance attached a copy of the Nevada Gaming Control Section covering the procedures for requesting a rule change.

(A number of people, including industry expert Walt Tyminski, publisher of the respected gaming newsletter *Rouge Et Noir*, suspected that Avance had trapped me. Instead of simply giving a grievance, I was forced into the more complicated process of trying to change the gaming regulations.)

Avance went on:

"We are aware of the New Jersey Supreme Court decision. We are also aware of other court decisions involving this issue."

He was referring to my Nevada cases, which were dismissed years ago. This statement did not augur well for our side.

A rule change? Now it had become complicated. A few weeks earlier, I met a bright, young San Francisco lawyer, Nancy Walters. She was fascinated with the case and agreed to do legal research for the nominal fee of $25 per hour.

I'd keep costs down by doing most of the work, writing the complaints and motions, making appearances, and delivering the oral arguments.

Nancy's fee was not only reasonable, but we would work together in such a way that I would know exactly how much chargeable time she would incur. This, by the way, is a huge loophole in the billing of many lawyers. (Ever notice how lawyers call and, to make a basic four-minute decision, keep a conversation going for 30 minutes or so to justify a charge for the entire time?)

Nancy and I drafted a petition to amend Regulation 28, which specified who may be excluded from casinos.

We argued that the regulation should be changed because casinos arbitrarily and capriciously exclude counters, violating their basic rights. We also cited the New Jersey Supreme Court decision.

*December 6, 1984*

We sent a letter to Avance requesting a change to Regulation 28, with a copy to Richard Bryan, the Governor of Nevada (a subsequent target of one of Johnny Carson's "Lighten Up" satires).

*January 21, 1985*

No word from the Commission for six weeks. I wrote to Paul Bible, Chairman, quoting a Nevada statute: "the commission shall within 30 days deny the request in writing or schedule the matter for action pursuant to this subsection."

In other words, we should have heard from the Commission by January 6, 1985.

To put pressure on the Commission, I also sent a copy of the package to the Attorney General, to inform them that the Commission had violated the Nevada statutes and could be subject to prosecution.

That attempt was laughable, as you will see.

*January 30, 1985*

The commission finally replied, claiming my letter wasn't received until January 28.

"The Commission is in the process of reviewing your Petition and you will be advised from this office within 30 days on the action to be taken. . ."

*February 19, 1985*

Good news! The Commission wrote, saying that they will consider my petition at a meeting in Vegas on June 20, 1985:

"At that time and place, the Commission will decide if it wants to proceed with your request for adoption of a regulation prohibiting the exclusion of card-counters from Nevada casinos."

For the first time in history, the Nevada Commission would address the card-counting issue!

I noted that the Commission wasn't deciding on the petition itself—it was addressing the procedural question of whether they should "proceed with (the) request." This distinction would later become significant.

Now it was time to go to work.

I put together a report for the hearing which was over 30 pages long, and included affidavits from card counters who were barred, read the Trespass Act, locked up in back rooms, arrested, and, in one case, physically beaten.

It included material from the New Jersey decision and arguments interpreting the Nevada statutes that would lead to the conclusion that skillful players cannot arbitrarily be barred.

Blackjack expert Arnold Snyder reviewed the material and made helpful suggestions.

The whole package took over a week—days and nights—to assemble. Inga and I stayed up all night copying the voluminous material on a Xerox.

The next day we would go to Vegas for the hearing.

Little did we suspect that we would be there almost four months.

Mr. Richard Hyte
Nevada State Gaming Control Board
Building D
4220 S. Maryland Parkway
Las Vegas, NV 89158

Dear Mr. Hyte:

I formally request a hearing before the Nevada State Gaming Control Board to consider the matter of whether I and other skilled blackjack players may be arbitrarily excluded from playing blackjack by Nevada casino management.

During the period, February 17 through 23, 1984, I was prevented from playing blackjack at four Lake Tahoe casinos:
Caesar's Tahoe
The High Sierra
Harvey's, and
Harvey's Inn
An affidavit describing each incident is included as Exhibit A.

In each case, the "barring" was based on the factor of skill at blackjack. One High Sierra Casino Shift Manager in fact stated, "We don't want you to play here. You're too good."

The Supreme Court Of New Jersey held, in Uston v. Resorts, on May 5, 1982, that:

- " The Casino Control Act (of New Jersey) precludes Resorts from excluding Uston for card counting", and

- " The common law right of an owner of a public place to exclude patrons is limited by a competing common law right of reasonable access to public places".

Pertinent pages of the syllabus of the Court's opinion are included as Exhibit B.

It is my opinion, and that of my attorney, Mr. Jonathan Rutledge, 2247 Union Street, San Francisco, CA 94123, that the the barring of skillful players by Nevada casinos is contrary to both the spirit and letter of the Nevada Statutes, the Constitution of the State of Nevada, and the Constitution of the United States.

Respectfully,

Kenneth S. Uston
2140 Taylor Street, # 1201/1202
San Francisco, CA 94133
(415) 775-7358

Letters exchanged with the Nevada Gaming Commission.

RICHARD H. BRYAN
*Governor*

STATE OF NEVADA

JAMES AVANCE, *Chairman*
PATRICIA BECKER, *Member*
RICHARD G. HYTE, *Member*
IRENE F. MORROS, *Executive Secretary*

GAMING CONTROL BOARD
4220 South Maryland Parkway
Building D
Las Vegas, Nevada 89158

April 2, 1984 TEL: (702) 731-3150

Mr. Kenneth S. Uston
2140 Taylor Street, #1201-1202
San Francisco, California 94133

Dear Mr. Uston:

We are in receipt of your letter of March 1, 1984. We are aware of the New Jersey Supreme Court decision. We are also aware of other court decisions involving this issue.

The hearing you request would be more appropriately handled as consideration of a proposed regulation. If you wish to pursue such action, it is our suggestion that you do so pursuant to NRS 463.145, a copy of which is attached for your review.

Thank you for your inquiry.

Very truly yours,

JAMES AVANCE
Chairman

JA/JAG:lw

Attachment

Letters exchanged with the Nevada Gaming Commission.

Mr. James Avance, Chairman
Nevada State Gaming Control Board
4220 South Maryland Parkway
Building D
Las Vegas, Nevada 89158

December 6, 1984

Dear Mr. Avance:

In accordance with the suggestion in your letter of April 2, 1984, I would like to request a hearing of the Control Board to consider a change to Regulation 28 of the Nevada Gaming Commission and Gaming Control Board, as outlined in the attached request and affidavit.

Thank you for your kind consideration.

Very truly yours,

Kenneth S. Uston
2140 Taylor St., #1201
San Francisco, CA 94133
(415) 775-7358

Letters exchanged with the Nevada Gaming Commission.

STATE OF NEVADA
NEVADA GAMING COMMISSION
1150 East William Street
Carson City, Nevada 89710
(702) 885-4701

GOVERNOR RICHARD H. BRYAN
Gaming Policy Committee, Chairman
ENE F. MORROS, Executive Secretary

PAUL A. BIBLE, Chairman
KENNETH R. GRAGSON, Member
BOB J. LEWIS, Member
JERRY LOCKHART, Member
JACK C. WALSH, Member

February 19, 1985

Mr. Ken Uston
2140 Taylor Street #1201
San Francisco, California 94133

Re: Petition for Amendment of NGC Regulation 28, "List of Excluded Persons," Pursuant to NRS 463.145(1)(d).

Dear Mr. Uston:

The purpose of this letter is to advise you that the subject matter raised in your January 28, 1985 petition for amendment of NGC Regulation 28 will be placed on the Nevada Gaming Commission's public agenda on June 20, 1985 at 10:30 a.m. in the Clark County School District Board Room at 2832 East Flamingo Road, Las Vegas, Nevada. At that time and place, the Commission will decide if it wants to proceed with your request for adoption of a regulation prohibiting the exclusion of card counters from Nevada casinos.

Should you have any further inquiry regarding this matter, please contact this office directly.

Very truly yours,

Irene F. Morros

Irene Morros
Executive Secretary

IFM/JCG/jr

Certified Mail No. P 665 698 832

Letters exchanged with the Nevada Gaming Commission.

STATE OF NEVADA GAMING COMMISSION HEARING

June 20, 1985 - Kenneth S. Uston - petitioner

SUMMARY

The Gaming Commission Should Consider

The Issue Of Whether To Amend Regulation 28

To Prohibit The Exclusion From Casinos Of Skillful Blackjack Players

(1) Excluding skillful blackjack players totally contradicts both the spirit and letter of Nevada Law:

a. The general statement of policy (N.R.S. 4630129(b))

b. The specific legislation, which not only identifies who may be excluded (N.R.S. 463.151), but also details specific procedures to be used for the exclusion process (N.R.S. 463.152, 463.153), including:

- the publication of a list of those excluded
- serving notice upon those excluded
- the right to a hearing to protest exclusion.

(2) Excluding skillful blackjack players totally contradicts both the spirit and letter of the regulations adopted by the Nevada Gaming Commission and the State Gaming Control Board:

a. The general statement of policy (Regulation 5.011)

b. The specific regulations, which not only identify who may be excluded (28.010), but also specify detailed procedures to be used for excluding people (28.030 through 28.080), including:

- the publication of a list of those excluded
- serving notice upon those excluded
- the right to a hearing to protest exclusion.

(3) Yet, barring of skilled blackjack players is currently a widespread practice among casinos.

(4) Further, more than merely barring, players are often read "The Trespass Act", threatening arrest if they return to the casino.

- Thus the Nevada criminal processes are involved in the barring process, and, in some cases, have led to arrests by the police, bookings, and court trials.

(5) Blackjack is widely accepted as a game of skill.

- Yet, skillful players are arbitrarily excluded
- Unskillful players, and degenerate, compulsive, or obsessive gamblers are allowed to play.

(6) Barring is:

- Arbitrary, because pitbosses bar players for what they think the player is thinking.

- Arbitary, because many pitbosses don't know how to count themselves. Thus, non-counters can easily be barred.

- Capricious, since pitbosses can readily use card-counting as an excuse to bar anyone they choose
  - this is the ultimate in arbitary, capricious exclusion, with absolutely no good cause or due process.

(7) The barring process is often abetted by a secret, but widely circulated, Griffin dossier which invades the privacy of individuals.

(8) Gaming establishments have absolutely no residual authority under either the Statutes or under common law to exclude skillful blackjack players.

(9) Given the Nevada statutes and relevant precedents, it is highly likely that any judicial review of this issue would conclude that casinos do not have the right to exclude persons they suspect are skillful players.

(10) Nevada casinos have ample counter-measures available to them to counteract all skillful blackjack players.

## RECOMMENDATION

Petitioner respectfully requests that Regulation 28.010 be amended by the addition of the following paragraph:

"Licensed gaming establishments may not exclude or deny reasonable access to their gaming premises or participation in all table games to any person without good cause. The fact that a person is suspected of skillfully playing under existing rules a game offered by licensees to the public, shall not, by itself, be considered good cause for exclusion."

# 4

# Finding Surprisingly Beatable Games in Las Vegas

Armed with legal files several feet thick, Inga and I flew to Vegas. We checked into the Frontier Hotel, where my Business Manager, Jerry Fuerle, who had flown in from New Jersey, was also staying.

The next morning was the Commission hearing, but it was now early evening. Obviously there was time to cruise around town and see what was happening.

I hadn't been to Vegas since the previous January's Consumer Electronics Show, five months earlier. On that trip, I'd won four grand (the electronic industry press picked up some rumors and, prone as the press is to "hyperbole," reported that it was $20,000).

Which brings me to journalistic accuracy. Most reporters I've dealt with take pains to stick to the facts. There are some, however, who won't hesitate to "enhance" a story.

One example: In December, 1979, the New Jersey Commission started an experiment in which the casinos were forced to deal to all blackjack players. The trade-off was that the casinos were allowed to shuffle after three decks (of the six decks then in use) were dealt, and could impose bet variation restrictions on players they suspected of card-counting.

A local reporter asked if she could sit at the table with me when I played. That was fine with me, and we went to Caesars Palace.

I put $30,000 on the table and started playing $100 to $1,000 a hand. A waitress came by. I asked her for a cup of coffee. A few minutes later she returned, embarrassed, and said:

"I'm sorry, sir, we can't serve you drinks."

I summoned a floorman, who told me:

"The casino manager said we can't serve drinks to counters."

This struck me as somewhat petty, and I muttered something to the reporter, like:

"I hope that cup of coffee costs them 30 grand."

After about three hours of play, I quit—up six or seven thousand.

The next day, the story appeared accurately in the reporter's newspaper.

The following day, a Philadelphia reporter, who never interviewed me, wrote his version of the incident. It went something like this:

"Ken Uston was in Caesars yesterday. They wouldn't serve him a cup of coffee, so he said, 'That's going to cost you $50,000.' After he won the $50,000, he headed for Resorts.

"The Resorts people heard Uston was coming and quickly put on a pot of coffee for him. He went easy on them, and took them for only 25 thousand."

A fascinating story except that it never happened.

It makes you wonder about those gambling stories about people like Nick the Greek. (One was, "He had two million on the craps table at midnight; the following morning he couldn't buy breakfast.")

Another example: The exalted *Time* Magazine did a piece about my gambling. In eight paragraphs, there were five errors. Ever since then, I've been reading newspapers and magazines with a jaundiced eye.

At any rate, there we were, ready to check out games on the Vegas Strip. Now, when the card-counter looks at a game, he watches for things that don't mean much to the average player. The most important things I look for are:

1. The rules of the game. Most people don't know this, but blackjack rules vary from casino to casino. For example, each of the follow-

ing clubs have rules that are different from the others: Ceasars Palace, Sahara, Barbary Coast, El Cortez, Horseshoe, Las Vegas Club, and Vegas World.

2. The number of decks. The fewer, the better.

3. How many cards are dealt, or "penetration," as it's called. The more cards dealt, the better.

4. The variation in bet size tolerated by the pit. Pros make money by betting more in favorable situations, and betting less in unfavorable situations. The greater the ratio, the higher the potential earnings.

5. How well they accept high action. Some clubs, like Caesars, have so many high-rollers that a black chip attracts little attention. In other clubs, like Circus Circus, betting green ($25) chips will attract pit bosses like flies.

After checking out the rather glum game (six decks, average penetration) at our host casino, the Frontier, we jumped into a cab, to tour the Strip from one end to the other.

We strolled past the tropical Hacienda fountain into their casino. They offered some shoe games (five decks), but several double deck games. Several dealers dealt far into the pack. One dealer dealt a double deck game down to less than 10 cards, phenomenally favorable penetration (he's tall, thin and hums while he deals—in case you're interested). I played a few hands, observing the pit; the bosses were all young; no recognizable faces.

Our next stop was the Tropicana, with its ornate cathedral ceiling covered with stained glass and its oval-shaped bar, fully stocked with unescorted young ladies.

The Trop had shoe games and several $25 minimum double deck games. Penetration was mixed.

I spotted Jack Newton, a boss I knew from another casino, and I quickly headed for the front door, ducking behind one pillar after another, like a soldier retreating under fire.

The blackjack player must always watch out for pit boss job shifts. Turnover is high in the gaming industry. More than once, I've been comfortably settled in a club only to be abruptly barred by a recently transferred boss who knew me from somewhere else.

The Marina announced "Single Deck 21" on a large sign in front of the hotel. Sure enough, there was one single deck game, located in a prominent spot near the entrance. All the other games used two or more decks.

Many Vegas casinos avoid offering single deck games, since they are aware how beatable they are. When a single deck game is allowed, it's closely policed by the bosses, who watch for suspicious bet variations and make sure that the dealers don't deal too far into the deck.

Many people assume there's no more single deck in Vegas. Not true. As I write this, there are single deck games in 21 Vegas casinos—all closely monitored.

There were lots of people watching the Marina single deck game—seven players, a dozen or so kibitzers crowded behind the players, and two wary bosses.

The game was obviously used to lure customers into the casino. The bosses chose to make sure the house wouldn't get hurt too badly; all the other blackjack games had a $500 maximum; at the single deck table, bets were limited to $200.

Then it was on to the Dunes. Good double deck games, dealt face up (good news for the counter, who sees more cards before playing his hand). I spotted Herb Nunez, the boss who "pulled me up" ten years ago at the Sands. Time to hide behind some more pillars.

The huge MGM used five decks, dealt three of them, and shuffled. Forget it. The MGM may have had the most extravagant topless show in town, but it was no place to make money.

Then, the pièce de résistance—Caesars Palace—to me, the finest casino-hotel in the world. Caesars also happens to be one of two Vegas casinos that let me play—as long as I don't bet more than $200.

Caesars is unique in the casino business. The suites, with mirrored ceilings and sunken tubs; the Grand Prix; world title boxing matches; the $5,000 per hand limit. Then there's the notorious Galleria bar—Vegans refer to it as the "Gonorrhea Bar," for reasons you can probably figure out.

Granted, Caesars is a bit overstated, but it does cater to every last need of the hedonist (of which I definitely am one). I guess you could call it elegant tackiness.

I remember drinking with the designer of Caesars casino, who told me, "An oval-shaped room gets men's juices flowing. So does a red and purple decor."

The Caesars image is enhanced by their logo—a portly older fellow lying back, being fed grapes by a scantily-clad nymphet.

Other casinos give you grapes; Caesars peels them.

By this time, Jerry and I were feeling no pain, but we continued on to the Flamingo, a club known for their use of the Griffin agency, the private detective agency that hounds card-counters—and circulates their pictures from casino to casino. Through the years, Griffin has cost me hundreds of thousands of dollars. Nevertheless, there were good double deck games at the Flamingo.

Then, to the Imperial Palace. Good games, but their bosses tend to cause counters to be jostled into a backroom, and occasionally arrested. Two card-counters who were hassled by the "IP," sued, and settled out-of-court for $100,000.

We continued our tour of the Strip:

Circus Circus—a grind joint (that is, caters to small bettors), with all single decks, fairly good penetration. Circus, incidentally, has become one of the most profitable casinos in Vegas.

The Sands—in its heyday home of the Sinatra Rat Pack, is still a high roller casino, with some double deck games, and lots of black chip players. It was *numero uno* until Caesars Palace opened its doors.

Theoretically I was still subject to arrest if I entered the Sands, since I'd been read the Trespass Act many years ago. Figuring the statute of limitations would apply, in we went. Just in case, I wore a baseball hat and sunglasses. It didn't work—one of the bosses spotted me.

I couldn't help thinking about the week-end I'd lost $71,000 here in 12 hours. These "negative swings," as we call them, happen all the time, because our edge is so tiny (about 1% over the house). Playing blackjack takes a lot of patience, internal fortitude, and the ability to take large losses in stride.

The Riv—the club we once hit so hard we're sure we put them in the red for three consecutive months. Now uninteresting with five decks.

The Sahara—I was recognized as soon as I walked in the door. We made a quick retreat, not even stopping for a drink.

The Sahara's always been tough on me. One time one of their floor managers wouldn't let me be the TV host for the first major blackjack tournament.

"You use Uston, and I won't let the cameras in the door."

He ranted and raved about me being a cheater—this from a guy who murdered his wife by shooting her in the stomach. Somehow he had "connections" and got off scot free.

Then it was off to downtown Vegas. At Binion's Horseshoe, I was spotted right away. This is the second club in town that lets me play; the catch: three rounds and shuffle. I responded by increasing the betting ratio and went ahead $1,500.

I was ready to cash out with a rack of green. The boss chided, "What's the matter, Kenny? You only beat us for a little over a thou."

Even though I had only $7,000 in my pocket, I foolishly took this as a challenge (to bet $1,000 per hand, the counter needs a bankroll of about $60,000 to have a 95% chance of winning).

I ran into a buzz saw and lost the seven grand in eight hands.

We checked out the Mint, Union Plaza and Sundance. All three clubs had highly beatable games.

The net impression from our bacchanalian journey: The town was looking like a candy store again.

There were, however, two big unknowns:

1. Even if I changed my appearance, how much heat would I get?

2. How much bet variation would the casinos stand for, now that just about every boss in town knew the game can be beaten?

(When we played years earlier, most bosses knew little about card-counting. Many thought that in the long run, the house *always* had to win. It was due to those marvelous misconceptions that our $650,000 came to us so quickly a few years back.)

Now I felt the same optimism that I did when I formed my $650,000 team. It looked like many casinos in town could be taken for quite a bit of money.

I said to Inga, "Maybe we'll stay in Vegas and play some blackjack."

# 5

# Getting Creamed by the Commission

Talk about hangovers. Up at 8 A.M. (ugh!), after two hours' sleep. Time to go to work. I put on a suit and tie, for the first time in months.

Our little entourage—Inga, Jerry, Jerry's girlfriend, and I—took a taxi to City Hall, a modern building in downtown Vegas.

We entered the City Council Chambers, a huge auditorium, with hundreds of seats. The Commissioners were sitting in high-backed chairs, behind a long, elevated podium, facing the audience. There were two TV crews, a battery of Control Board employees, and several dozen spectators.

A couple of reporters approached me and asked questions.

I felt cautiously optimistic. This was no small behind-the-scenes smoky backroom political meeting. We were to receive a legitimate hearing in full view of the public and the media. Perhaps equitable justice might be dispensed here after all.

There were dozens of items on the docket, and we were far down the list. I watched and listened, to get an idea of how this Commission operated.

It soon became obvious that the Nevada Gaming Commission exerted enormous power over people's lives. We listened as the Commission made decisions on dealers' jobs, executives' careers, and the licensing of multi-million dollar casinos. (This was the very commission that refused to grant Frank Sinatra a casino license.)

One fellow, a dealer who had been arrested, pleaded to get his license back. He brought his parole officer to attest that he had reformed. The Commission voted for him.

A former casino executive had a record of alcoholism and outrageous crimes —trespassing, rape, burglary, just about everything short of murder. He claimed to be a five-year member of AA and a born-again Christian and pleaded for reinstatement.

Permission granted.

The owner of the Royal Las Vegas, Joe Slyman (I would soon be playing in his casino), pled to keep his casino open. He'd violated sections of the Casino Control Act and had been fined. He was also accused of transferring funds between accounts to avoid creditors.

Permission to operate granted.

It seemed to me that the Commissioners were in a good mood. Would that augur well for us?

A huge Canadian corporation wanted permission to open a casino, Bourbon Street, in just three days. The company had flown in a host of executives in three-piece suits to testify.

When they announced one of the names, I cringed. James Avance, the Chairman of the Control Board, who had written me suggesting that I file for a regulation change, was wearing another hat. He had left the Board to become Chief Executive of the Bourbon Street Casino—at a big increase in salary.

In New Jersey, a Commission employee must wait two years before working for a casino. There's no such rule in Nevada. I took the Avance transfer as a bad sign—an example of the Nevada ol' boy network in action.

The Commissioners asked some tough questions about Bourbon Street's financial resources. The questioning was so probing, and the responses so weak, that logic would dictate that the license be denied.

The Bourbon Street execs were sweating, as the Commissioners' questions kept implying that their financial backing was inadequate. Hundreds of jobs and millions in investments hung on the decision.

It was time to vote. The license was granted unanimously. As the

Bourbon Street people filed out of the chambers, one executive wiped his brow, and murmured an audible, "Whew." He meant it. These guys were shook up. (My natural skepticism led me to believe that some of this drama may have been orchestrated, in sort of a "let the record reflect that the Commission really delved into this matter.")

Time for lunch. Then another half dozen cases were heard.

It was four P.M. when my case was finally called.

I stood up, identified myself, and addressed the Commission:

"Mr. Chairman. I submitted the petition for the modification of either Regulation 28 or some other change in the regulations. I am not pursuing this as a matter of selfish interest.

"The issues involve the basic reputation of the casinos, of Las Vegas, Reno, Lake Tahoe, and the State of Nevada, and the welfare, I believe, of many citizens who reside both in Nevada and elsewhere."

I continued with my presentation, perspiring under the heat of the intense TV spotlights.

I had no idea what opposition I'd encounter. I soon found out.

The Chairman turned to three men in suits, sitting together in the front row, and said:

"You are obviously here to support Mr. Uston, correct?"

I was confused. Then I understood the chairman's sarcasm when one of the men stood up and identified himself as the lawyer for the Nevada Resort Association, which represents every major casino in Vegas.

He argued against me, quoting from decisions in my abortive Vegas cases of years ago. He concluded:

"NRS 463.151 gives rise to no affirmative obligation by the State of Nevada to compel gaming establishments to admit persons thought to be card counters."

Shannon Bybee, a top executive from the Golden Nugget, and an old foe from the New Jersey legal battles, was one of the adversarial triumvirate. He, too, argued against my position.

Then the Nevada political network made itself heard. Harry Wald, a high level MGM executive, took the microphone and said:

"I represent the MGM Grand Hotel. I am also authorized to speak on behalf of Summa Corporation, Hilton Hotels, Caesars Palace, Tropicana, the Boyd properties, the Mint, Four Queens, Las Vegas Club and the Union Plaza."

Translation:

"I speak for just about every major casino in this town. If you guys want to get better jobs in this town some day . . ."

As Walt Tyminski prognosticated in an article in the March, 1985, issue of *Rouge Et Noir* which predicted I'd have a tough time:

"The industry has a lot of clout in Nevada. You have to remember that the people that work for the Gaming Control Board today are likely to be looking for a job eventually. In Nevada the likely future employer is a casino."

In addition to James Avance's move to Bourbon, Patricia Becker, a Commissioner when I first filed my complaint, left the Commission to become legal counsel for Harrah's casino.

Under these circumstances, how can Commissioners possibly make objective decisions which directly affect the profits of the casino industry? It was worse than the Pentagon admirals who got jobs with defense contractors when they retired. Even the Nevada Governor once complained that there should be a two-year waiting period, as in Atlantic City, before Commission employees could work for a casino.

Commissioner Peccole didn't think I had come to the right place:

"I'm having a real problem with whether or not we even have the jurisdiction to come in at this stage. . . ."

He told me that I should approach the legislature to make the change I wanted.

That was a glum alternative. The Nevada legislature meets every other year and had just adjourned. Thus, I would have had to wait two more years.

I was relieved when Chairman Bible dissented:

"I disagree with Commissioner Peccole . . . I feel that the authority of the Commission is sufficiently broad [to deal with this issue]."

Chairman Bible made a surprising admission:

"I might also note for the record that years ago I read the Thorpe book [a blackjack book] and there was a period of time when I even tried my hand at it. It's not easy to stay alert for very long doing that."

After some more discussion, Commissioner Lewis turned toward the Chairman:

"I'd move to authorize you to deny the position or the petition that's been submitted to us by Ken Uston and that you deny that petition in writing."

The secretary called the role.

"Mr. Lewis?"

"Aye."

"Mr. Gragson?"

"Aye."

"Mr. Peccole?"

"Aye."

"Mr. Lockhart?"

"Aye."

(I sensed that one commissioner was sympathetic with our position. During my presentation he occasionally nodded affirmatively when I made a point. When they called his name to vote, he lowered his eyes, and responded softly, as if his heart wasn't in it. But after all, he'd be looking for a better job someday, too.)

"Mr. Bible?"

"Aye."

Chairman Bible said:

"Thank you. It was an interesting presentation."

That was that. I hadn't expected to win; we even lost at the Commission level in New Jersey (by a vote of 4 to 1). But I was hoping the decision against us wouldn't be unanimous.

I was obviously disheartened when interviewed by reporters after the hearing. But as I told them, "The battle's not over yet."

Now it was on to the courts.

# 6

# Forming a $53,000 Blackjack Team

I had no intention of getting into another blackjack effort, but the Vegas games were too enticing.

A chance meeting made the decision for me. I received a call from Bob, a fellow who wanted to take a blackjack lesson.

Bob lived in Los Angeles and had been playing low stakes blackjack in Vegas with a concealed computer for the past several years. He had limited success and a small bankroll (around $15,000).

A blackjack computer plays better than the best ten card-counters in the world, playing in concert. The computer keeps track of how many of each card denomination is played and how many of each remain in the deck. Us mere mortals, on the other hand, simply use a plus-minus count. We know the proportion of types of cards (high or low) remaining to be played. There's a huge difference.

For example, I might know that there is roughly half a deck left (26 cards) and that there are far more than the normal number of 8 tens left in the deck.* I would also know how many aces are left, because I count aces separately (on my feet).

The computer, on the other hand, would know, for example, that there are exactly 25 cards remaining: 11 tens, 3 aces, 3 deuces, 2 threes, no fours or fives, 3 sixes, 1 seven, 1 eight and 1 nine.

Not only that, the computer would make optimum use of its information.

Back in 1977, I organized a computer team which won $135,000 in six weeks. With the computers, we won 80% of the time. When we play conventionally, we win 60% of the time.

The fellow who developed our computers started selling them. Dozens of players bought them and began using them in Nevada and Atlantic City.

Concealed computers became so prevalent that Harrah's lawyers spearheaded an effort to make their use in casinos illegal. They began their lobbying in early 1985. By spring, the legislature passed a bill making the use of computers a felony. Shortly after, the governor signed the bill, to become effective July 1, 1985. First offenders would be subject to a fine of up to $10,000 and 10 years in jail. They weren't fooling around.

It's funny how fast the Nevada executive and legislative arms can move when the casino industry wants something. I do agree that using a concealed blackjack computer gives the player an unfair advantage. Using your brain is an entirely different matter, though.

It was June 20, 1985. Computers weren't illegal yet.

Bob and I had dinner. It was obvious that he knew what he was talking about. I suggested that we might make some money together before the July 1st blackjack computer ban went into effect. I said I might consider putting up some money.

As I listened to Bob, I thought of other players who had been after me to start a team.

At the time, I had nothing else to do except work on the lawsuit—definitely a part-time effort.

I decided the time had come. Uncertain of the climate in Nevada toward high-rolling counters, I would hedge and invest only a nominal $25 thousand.

*When there is a disproportionate number of tens (and aces) remaining in the deck, the cards favor the player. When the reverse is true, the cards favor the house.

I'd organize the team, and do a little playing myself. The goal—make a few bucks, get back into the swing of things, and have some fun; Vegas *is* the partyingest town in the country.

I told Bob, "Let's give it a shot."

## The Plan

To augment the firepower of Bob's computer, I'd have several other counters playing as well. Thus we would get into the "long run" quicker. This would reduce the fluctuations in our bankroll—by far the biggest ulcer factor in playing blackjack.

Statistically, having many counters is similar to a casino having a number of blackjack tables. When the Dunes first opened up, it had few tables; its blackjack operation often ran in the red for days on end. Contrast this with the huge Harrah's and Resorts casinos, which have so many tables that they rarely, if ever, have a losing day.

Bob could use the computer until July 1. We'd also start with two conventional counters. I'd play in disguise. We'd also have Tony, a fellow who had been calling me for the past year and had sounded impressive over the phone.

Neither Bob, nor Tony, nor I would play the big money. We'd all bet as little as possible, and "call" plays—that is, give signals to Big Players (BP's), which would tell them how much to bet and how to play their hands.

This was a ploy I'd used in the past in Nevada and Atlantic City to good advantage. It takes the heat off both the counter and the BP:

The counter appears to be just another small bettor. If his signals are subtle, he draws little or no heat from the pit.

The BP is a high-roller, but he's drinking and not watching the other players' cards. If he puts on a good "act," bantering with the dealer and carrying on as if he's just out having some fun, he's rarely suspected of "doing something."

I knew no one had used the BP concept to any great extent. It takes a lot of organization and advanced scheduling, and there are other disadvantages as you will see. The bosses hadn't had much exposure to this technique. It appeared we'd be able to pull the wool over their eyes for some time.

By the way, being a BP is about the most enjoyable—and easiest—

job there is. All the BP has to do is read the counter's signals accurately. He can joke with players, dealers and pit bosses, seemingly throw piles of hundred dollar bills around, flirt with women, order numerous cocktails, and generally have a good time.

Being a BP gets the juices flowing; it's a "Mission Impossible" adventure; he's putting something over on the bosses. No one in the casino knows what's going on except the counter and the BP.

People will line up to be a BP. Even though BP's don't earn as much as the counters (they get 10% of what they win), they can live out the fantasy of being rich big shots in the casino. They're catered to by dealers, cocktail waitresses, and pit bosses, comped to every service the casinos can provide, pursued by women, and in general treated like kings.

A few years ago, I was a BP at the Sahara Tahoe. A counter, Jan, was signaling to me how much to bet and how to play the hands. I was drinking double vodka-grapefruits, and, as I played, I was chatting with the Casino Manager, Paul Syphus.

When I saw Jan's signal for a big bet, I'd ask Paul, "How many hands of $500? You tell me."

Then whatever Paul said, I'd do.

When Jan signaled a negative count, I'd feign preoccupation with a lady at the next table, a cocktail waitress, or some other distraction, and ignore my table, not even playing. I'd chase down a passing cocktail waitress for a napkin, a Kleenex, a straw, another drink, anything, leaving the table temporarily until Jan flashed a "big bet" signal. Then I'd come back in with a $500 bet.

Once, with a $500 bet out, and supposedly distracted from the game by talking to Paul, I picked up my cards a few inches. Jan could see them, but I couldn't. Jan signaled, "Stand," before I had a chance to see the cards.

I turned to Paul and said, "I'm gonna stand on this hand, sight unseen."

Paul laughed, no doubt thinking, "This guy's not only a sucker, he's insane."

That one play went a long way to ensure that I played at the Sahara for weeks.

In short, if executed with imagination, the BP concept works wonders.

There are disadvantages to the BP approach.

First, flexibility in the casino is drastically reduced. Once the two players are established at a table, they risk exposure when they both change tables if, say, the dealer starts shuffling too frequently.

Second, using a BP, of course, means the counter can never play alone ("head on"). The fewer players at the table, the greater the average earnings. The head-on player often plays 200 hands per hour, the optimum earning situation.

With a BP, there are usually more than two players at the table. The counter is less likely to be associated with the BP if there are other players at the table. A full table with seven players averages only 75 hands per hour. Thus, with a BP, we've got to play almost three times as long to earn as much, on average, as we would if we were playing head on.

Third, the percentage advantage over the house is greater with fewer players. There are several technical reasons for this. For example, with fewer players, the proportion of unprofitable hands dealt "off the top" (i.e., from a freshly-shuffled deck) is lower; thus the proportion of advantageous hands is greater.

Fourth, to avoid attracting attention, the counter should not vary his bet or make advanced plays. These restrictions prevent him from having an edge over the house—in fact, in games with more than one deck, the house has the edge over our counter. This, of course, costs the team money, especially if it is playing at $25 minimum tables. For this reason, we rarely play $100 minimum tables when we use a BP.

## Recruiting

It was time to get the team together. Assembling a team always reminds me of the movie *The Sting*, where experts with various "specialties" were summoned, from all over the country, to ply their trade in a gambling operation.

In addition to Inga (who would be a BP) and myself, I had six other people in mind. The dramatis personae:

### The Innocuous Student

Bob looked like the computer-hacker that he was. He was pint-sized, had a squeaky voice, and wore glasses as thick as the bottoms of Coke bottles. A graduate of Dartmouth, he was planning to get an advanced degree in math at the University of California at Irvine. Bob was paranoid to a fault. He was convinced pit bosses were on to him, and he saw Griffin agents behind every pillar. He was obsessed with concealing his Vegas address, and would drive a complex, circuitous route on his way home after sessions.

Bob had been barred six times in the past year, and his picture was in the Griffin Mug Book. We'd have to be careful where we used him.

## The South Philly Kid

Tony had been calling me up over the past year, pestering me for a spot on one of my teams. I'd never met him. I did know that he spoke like a Brooklyn hood, which was definitely not an attribute of the typical card-counter.

Despite this, Tony was a highly trained player; he used the Uston Advanced Point Count (APC), one of the more difficult counts to master. He claimed he could count down a six-deck shoe in 90 minutes, which is almost unheard of. He'd thoroughly memorized the 150 numbers necessary to know how to make advanced blackjack plays (sample: with a count of plus 5, you split tens against a 6, and so on).

I called Tony. I felt even better about him when he said, "In the last four months, I won forty grand in AC. When I'm not playing, I practice at least four hours a day."

I asked Tony how much he'd put in our bank. (I've always preferred that all players have some money in the bank—they tend to work harder when their own money's at risk.)

Tony wanted to put in $12,000.

I told Tony to fly out as soon as he could. He said, "See you the day after tomorrow."

## The Vegas Poker Player

I'd known Robert, a writer, for years. I first met him when he interviewed me for an article for *Signature*, the Diner's Club magazine. (I would often relate how we were served a sour bottle of wine while dining at Caesars Palace Court. The only time in my life I ever rejected a bottle of wine was while being interviewed by a writer for a national gourmet magazine.)

Robert graduated as a top scholar from Harvard and became a mathematics professor. He was destined to have a brilliant career. Then he dropped out and took a lengthy trip around the world. He was now living a hand-to-mouth existence in Vegas, ekeing out a modest living playing poker. Robert was fifty, had sparse, gray hair, a pot belly, and smoked and drank more than he should.

Robert would be a convincing BP. He was known in town as a losing blackjack player—and the money he suddenly "came into" could easily be explained the result of his having played lucky at poker.

I called Robert. He jumped at the chance. Robert was to become one of our very best BP's.

## The Street Smart New Yorker

The Turf Lounge in the Jockey Club is a convenient meeting ground. Every night at cocktail hour, there are a dozen hard-core drinkers, drawn mostly from the hustling time-share salesmen that work there during the day.

One of the drinkers, Frank, looked Italian (he was) and sounded like he was from the Lower East Side (he was).

Frank wasn't a condo salesman, but always seemed to have hundred dollar bills to throw around. He was outgoing, friendly, and was generally the one to buy the most rounds. His dress was best described as Vegas Garnish; he wore a lot of gold.

Frank laughed easily and loudly and liked to make others laugh with his endless supply of jokes. It seemed to me that he would put on a terrific "act" for the bosses.

I asked Frank if he'd be interested.

He replied "Are you kidding? When do we start?"

## Rambo

I'd used Barry as a BP in Vegas before. He was six feet two, looked like a weight lifter, had arms like tree trunks, and moved and talked like a red-neck cop. Barry had a deep voice, could drink like a fish, and on occasion would get into bar brawls, which is why we came to call him Rambo.

On a previous team, he played the Golden Nugget as a BP for

twelve straight hours, had about two dozen vodka grapefruits, and never missed a signal. He was known in town for his love of the grape.

### The San Franciscan Businessman

Neil was a gentleman from The Old School. Quite proper at all times, he had a refined, gentle voice and wore European-tailored suits. Neil, a retired businessman, could have passed for a United Nations diplomat.

Neil had known about my blackjack exploits and was fascinated with the idea of beating casinos at one of their own games. He had always been intrigued with the idea of becoming a BP.

Neil wouldn't carry on boisterously at the blackjack tables. His "act" would be that of a quiet, wealthy (which he was) gentleman who happened to love to play blackjack. He'd be a convincing high-roller.

I called Neil and told him all signals were "Go."

The following week, he was on a plane to Vegas.

With these eight people, I felt that we had the nucleus of a strong team. As had been the case in the past, some of the "hiring" decisions were good; some were bad. As we went along, some people would leave us—and new faces would join us.

# 7

# Using Blackjack Computers in the Casinos

Talking to Bob brought back reminiscences of the first blackjack computer team I organized, nearly 8 years before.

While 90% of our earnings have been made from "cerebral" blackjack over the years, the money never rolled in at a faster rate than during the brief period we used eight concealed blackjack computers.

## The First Practical Blackjack Computer

In January, 1977, I was running a team of blackjack players from my condos at the Jockey Club (still my Vegas headquarters). We'd had a good 1976, winning $650,000 in the last eight months of that year.

One day, I received an intriguing call from a scientist I'll call Peter, who lived in what was to become known as Silicon Valley, in Northern California.

"I've got a computer that plays better blackjack than any counter can. You can wear it, undetected, inside a casino."

Through the years I've gotten lots of calls from cranks with money-making schemes. But there was something in Peter's voice that led me to believe he was on the level.

I told Peter to catch the next plane to Vegas.

When I saw the computer, I knew Peter was on to something. However, I felt the design was impractical. The computer required the player to input information using both feet, by activating four tiny toe switches built into a specially-constructed pair of shoes.

Peter and I worked together and finally came up with a more workable design, in which the operator could input the information with his fingers. We code-named the computer "George."

Peter returned to the Bay Area and assembled the new model.

The computer itself was crammed inside a plastic casing about half the size of a pack of cigarettes. It was powered by a battery pack. An output "tapper" buzzed to provide the player with information. The revised input device was a series of switches built onto a plastic mounting (curved to fit around the thigh) and fastened by an Ace Bandage.

George was uncanny. As I've said, counters keep track only of the types of cards that are played; George kept track of each denomination.

After each play, George went through thousands of calculations to determine the precise advantage enjoyed by the house (or the player). George then signaled us how much to bet, to the nearest $100 (we assumed a starting bankroll of $50,000).

George also told us how to play each hand—that is, whether to hit, stand, double down or split pairs. Thousands of calculations were performed before these decisions were made and then signaled to the user.

Because George knew how many of each card denomination was left in the deck (or decks), we'd often be called on to make weird plays. We were told to hit hard 17, something no player in his right mind would do. On occasion, George would tell us to do such strange things as split 6's against an ace, and double down on 12, 13 and 14. We thought this was terrific. The pit bosses would think our players were crazed.

The input device was strapped around the player's left leg with the Ace Bandage (we had to cut out the left pockets of our pants to get to it). The device had four switches, each activated by a finger. The output tapper vibrated, using a series of Morse Code-like dots and dashes, signaling us how much to bet and how to play our hands.

Peter and I began the arduous task of training me to use George. Many times during the training, I became discouraged and doubted that I could operate George rapidly and accurately enough for use in actual casino play. But each day I gradually improved. After ten days, Peter and I agreed it was time for a casino test.

On February 1, 1977, George and I took a cab to the Golden Gate casino in downtown Vegas for a trial run. To my knowledge, this was the first time a really viable blackjack computer had been used in a casino. (There had been several previous attempts, *e.g.*, bulky models under raincoats, eyeglasses with flashing lights, etc.)

I played for several hours, betting only $5 to $50, and came out $193.50 ahead. The statistics, of course, were meaningless, given the small sample size of a few hundred hands or so, but we had proved that George could work.

Now we began training "computer operators"—people who pushed the buttons as they kept up with the cards that were dealt. To prevent detection from the pit bosses, Peter also devised a small radio transmitter that sent signals from the computers to a receiving unit-tapper, mounted in the BP's right shoe.

Thus each of our BP's had a "magic" pair of shoes that told how to bet and play his hands perfectly—beyond the ability of any human. All he had to do was sit at the table, hold his cards so the operator could see them, and follow the signals he received from the "tapper."

My Jockey Club condos became transformed into electronic workshops. Everywhere were battery chargers, soldering irons, wires, and "magic" shoes filled with mysterious electronic components.

My job was to recruit and administer the team. Peter handled the electronics. Our team soon grew to sixteen people: eight computer operators and eight BP's.

Finally one Monday morning, at two A.M. we were ready. We'd decided to play graveyard shift because there'd be fewer players at the table (thus more hands per hour, and a higher earnings potential).

I took $45,000 out of the safety deposit box. We dispatched three teams (an operator and a BP) to three single-deck clubs: the Stardust, Sahara and Circus Circus.

Because I was known in just about every club in Vegas, I manned the phone in the condo, as team coordinator. If a counter had a problem, such as a malfunctioning George or weak batteries, he'd call in. Then I'd dispatch another counter and call the BP and tell him to take a break until the substitute arrived on the scene. (The casinos' efficient paging system was enormously helpful to our team; whenever I wanted to talk to a BP, I'd page "Mr. Tiny George," a veiled reference to our miniature electronic helper.)

That night we won $6,500. Over the next three weeks we won about 80% of the time, far better than our average of 60% playing "manual" blackjack. After five weeks our team was up to $130,000. I particularly remember Peter's son, our youngest member, fingering the 21 hundred-dollar bills he'd won in the first three weeks. He kept staring at the bills, not quite believing they were really his.

At first, the casinos loved our BP's, whom they viewed as high-rollers bound to lose a bundle. One time our BP's were comped into the Stardust, Caesars, the Riviera and the Marina, all at the same time. They were living the life of Riley, staying in lavish suites, enjoying ringside show seats and gourmet meals—and making money while doing it!

Our BP's were running up literally thousands of dollars in "comped" services, which the casinos were more than happy to provide. One evening, we had four BP's at four separate tables in Caesars lavish Palace Court restaurant, all on the house. Naturally they pretended not to know each other.

One BP, comped into a Hilton suite, really broke it off. One night we had a team banquet, ordering eight dinners from room service, complete with hors d'oeuvres, appetizers, and desserts, to say nothing of five bottles of booze and four bottles of wine. Over the course of four days, this BP ordered ten more bottles; he took them when he checked out and stocked up his personal bar at home.

As we kept winning, the heat gradually started to come down. Strange men were following our players out of casinos. Bosses were overheard talking about guys with "hands in their pockets." One BP was barred from the Hilton:

"We don't want your action in here any more." Worse yet, the computer-counter was barred, too. Were they catching on to our modus operandi?

We decided to go north and let Vegas cool down for a while.

I drove up north with $70,000, and rented a house high in the hills of Tahoe, where we set up our electronics workshop on a ping-pong table in the attic. We trained for a few days, until finally, on a sunny day, early in May, 1977, I dispatched four teams of two people each: two to the huge Sahara casino, one to Harrah's, and one to Harvey's Wagon Wheel. The BP's bet up to $1,000 per hand. The first day we won $20,000.

The next day, May 14, 1977, four hours after the teams had left for the casinos, the phone rang. As I picked it up, I was fully prepared to hear that we had won another $30,000 or so.

"Ken, this is Steve."

"Hi. How're things going?"

"I'm in jail."

Steve had been operating his computer in Harrah's and was suddenly jostled into a back office by two burly security guards. They stripped him and found him full of wires and electronic devices, no doubt convinced he was some kind of terrorist.

They apparently called the other casinos, because two other teammates were arrested. The police must have had some difficulty coming up with an applicable violation. The charge they tried was "bunko steering"; we were accused of luring an unsuspected individual into an illicit gambling game. At any rate, I posted the $6,000 bail ($2,000 each). We got out of town—fast.

In retrospect, it was obvious that placing $1,000 bets at three clubs at the Lake simultaneously drew far more attention than it did in Vegas. Even a $100 bet at the Lake attracts attention from the pit.

The Casino Control Commission was totally baffled by our equipment. They didn't know what to make of it and decided to ship it to the FBI in Washington, D.C., for analysis. Five months later the FBI sent the computers back, reporting that in their opinion the computers were not "cheating devices." All charges were dropped.

No, we didn't try to resume the operation, largely because one of the people arrested was Peter's son. Peter had been getting a lot of pressure from his wife to get out of blackjack—to do something "legitimate"—and he decided to quit. I didn't pursue the issue, since in the meantime I had returned to the world of cerebral blackjack.

Yes, sometimes I feel as if I blew it. If I'd been content to have our team generate only $10,000 or $15,000 per week, chances are we'd have continued to play—at least until July 1, 1985. On the other hand, it has always been my philosophy in playing blackjack that if there's an opportunity, you should capitalize on it immediately and to the fullest. Otherwise, it will evaporate or someone else will take advantage of it.

No, I don't look back (often). There are too many things going on now. It was an adventuresome experience—and 135 grand ain't hay.

Since then, other players have bought and used hidden computers. Peter continued to manufacture and sell computers (for $4,000), complete with all necessary accessories—even a training manual (written by the widely known blackjack writer Arnold Snyder).

Several of my former teammates bought updated versions of George, which Peter called "David." These were used in both Atlantic City and Nevada.

Peter developed another type of computer called a "shuffle-tracking" computer, code-named "Thor." Thor, an expanded version of David, was ingenious. It would tell the player the types of cards in different portions of a pack of cards—before they were dealt!

The operators would enter the value of the cards as they were slid into the discard rack. The operator would track the dealer's shuffle pattern and the location of the cut. With this data entered accurately, Thor would be able to determine the types of cards that were in different portions or "segments" of the newly shuffled shoe.

Thor would tell the players how much to bet (for example, if a segment rich in 10 values was about to be dealt, the computer would call for a large bet, to take advantage of this positive situation).

Better yet, if the operator was given the cut, he would know exactly where to cut the pack so 10-valued cards were toward the front. Then the operator could make large bets off the top of the shoe, an action which would clearly show he was not a card-counter.

Eventually dozens of players were using Georges, Davids, Thors, and other computers in the casinos. Several enterprising electronic geniuses went so far as to "rip off" Peter's invention and sell counterfeit versions.

Gradually players began getting pulled into back rooms, searched and found with hidden computers. Finally the casinos had enough. They lobbied the Legislature, which soon passed the law prohibiting the use of casino computers.

The team that I formed in June, 1985, would be one of the very last to use a blackjack computer in Nevada—legally, at any rate.

## The Last Legal Blackjack Computer

Bob brought his computer over to my room at the Frontier. He had one of Peter's revised models, called "David."

David, a confusing mass of wires and multi-colored electronic components of all sizes and shapes, was mounted in the hollow heels of a pair of over-sized shoes. Bob ran wires up one leg and down the other. Built in to the shoes were little metal input switches, mounted on hinges just above and below the toes, which moved up and down.

Bob slipped a battery pack into another opening in the shoes and snapped it in place. A miniature tapper had been built in, flush with the top of the instep, so it could signal Bob by vibrating against the bottom of his foot.

It took Bob half an hour to don the equipment and get it working properly. Because of my skepticism toward toe switches, Bob knew he had to convince me that he could operate David accurately.

When Bob was ready, I dealt some hands to him. He played rapidly and, except for the faint buzzing I could hear in the silence of the hotel room, there was nothing unusual about the way he played.

At the end of each deck, I held out four or five cards. Bob asked the computer how many cards were left and what their denominations were.

At first he was inaccurate, which I attributed to nervousness. After working for two hours, it was a close call. Bob was fairly accurate, but not nearly up to the standards of the George players I'd previously worked with.

Bob kept saying, "Maybe my batteries are weak."

After another hour or so, it seemed to me that, despite occasional errors, Bob still had an acceptable edge over the house. I decided to go with him.

Bob would play single-deck games primarily, because the power of computer play is far stronger when only 52 cards are in play. We would concentrate on Circus Circus, Holiday Strip, Sundance, Marina, the Horseshoe, the Mint, and Westward Ho.

Bob would signal our BP's physically, rather than use George's radio transmitters, which were not available to us. So he had a lot to do when he was in the casino:

—operate the computer
—make his own bets and play his hands, smoothly
—interpret the output from David, and
—signal the BP what to do.

It was sort of like rubbing your stomach, patting your head, reciting the alphabet backwards, and tap-dancing—all at the same time.

Since the BP would be betting up to $1,000 per hand, accuracy was essential.

We had some heavy-duty training and practice ahead of us.

**Appendix**

The language of the computer law makes it clear the state is not fooling around. For just a first offense, there's a minimum of one year in the State Pen!

Here's how the law reads:

"It is unlawful for any person at a licensed gaming establishment to use, or possess with the intent to use, any device to assist:

1. In projecting the outcome of the game;
2. In keeping track of the cards played;
3. In analyzing the probability of the occurrence of an event, relating to the game,
4. In analyzing the strategy for playing or betting to be used in the game, except as permitted by the commission."

What bothers me about this language is whether "any device" could be considered a basic strategy table (which has at times been given out free by casinos), a pencil, or your playing chips (to keep track of the count).

Worse yet, "in keeping track of the cards played" I count aces by moving my foot to different positions. Are my feet devices?

Could a player go to jail for a year for counting aces with his feet?

Here are the penalties:

"(a) For the first offense, by imprisonment in the state prison for not less than 1 year nor more than 10 years, or by a fine of not more than $10,000, or by both fine and imprisonment.

"(b) For a second or subsequent violation of any of these provisions, by imprisonment in the state prison for not less than 1 year nor more than 10 years, and may be further punished by a fine of not more than $10,000.

"Any person who attempts, or two or more persons who conspire, to violate any provisions . . . each shall be punished by imposing the penalty provided . . . for the completed crime, whether or not he personally played any gambling game or used any prohibited device."

These guys mean business.

DO NOT UNDER ANY CIRCUMSTANCES USE A BLACKJACK COMPUTER IN THE STATE OF NEVADA!

# 8

# The 1985 Blackjack Training Camp

The headquarters for previous teams was the Jockey Club, a convenient non-casino location. It is on the Strip across from the Aladdin. Our former group had grown so large that we eventually needed four condos there.

Team members pretend not to know each other in the casinos. They cannot be seen together by casino personnel. If one teammate has been "made," others seen with him would draw heat "by proxy." Vegas bosses were notorious for resorting to "guilt by association."

The Jockey Club was fairly safe territory. It was inhabited mostly by out-of-towners and non-casino locals. (I later found out that the Hilton casino manager was living there, but this was no real risk—the Hilton, with their frequently-shuffled six-deck game, was not on our hit list.)

Our new team would also work out of two Jockey Club condos. When I walked into my condo, #558, it was like déjà vu. The condo was a replica of #658, the one I'd lived in for years, running teams. It was exciting to think that, after all these years, we'd soon be back in action again.

The first order of business was to train Bob and two BP's, Robert and Frank, so we could start using David. There were only eight days left before the computer-felony law went into effect.

## The Signals

We got a blackjack table, chips, a dealing shoe, and 30 decks of cards.

The first decision that had to be made was what signals to use. The BP needs to know two things, at two different times, during the course of play:

—How much to bet, after the completion of each round ("betting signals").

—How to play his hand, when he's received his cards and it's his turn to play ("playing signals").

In the past, the counter signaled bet size to the BP, by the placing of his bet in different locations on the betting "square" (sometimes the "square" is a circle, a wheel, or a casino logo). We'd use this same technique.

In the past, for playing signals, we used the location of the counter's right hand to tell the BP what to do:

—Hit, if the counter's hand riffled his chips.

—Stand, if the counter's hand was on the table, away from his chips.

—Double down or split, if the counter's hand was drawn back to the edge of the blackjack table.

But these playing signals weren't exactly a secret. I'd used them to signal a *60 Minutes* staffer when we went out to play counter and BP for millions of American viewers. Thus it seemed obvious these signals had to change.

A few days earlier, a retired blackjack player, barred all over town, came over and we got to discussing signals. He showed me the signals he had used. They were far more subtle than the old ones, and just as easy to read. I decided to go with them.

### *Betting Signals*

The BP would know how to bet by the placement of the counter's bet on the betting square.

He'd bet from 1 to 8 chips, as follows:

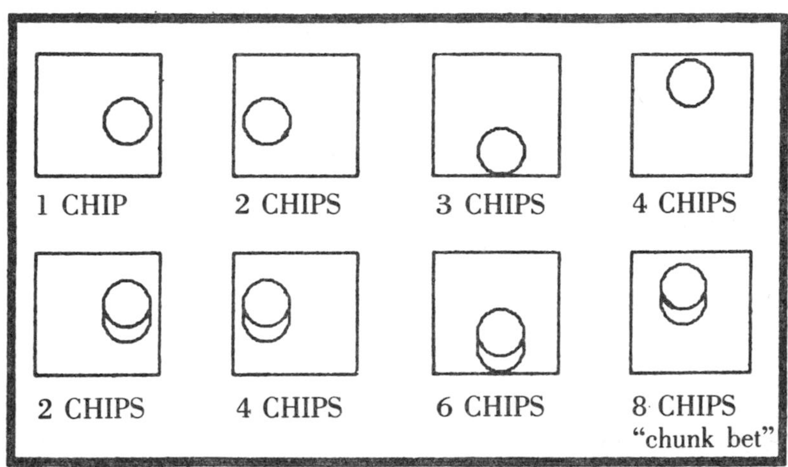


By expressing the bet in number of chips, we'd be able to play at different betting levels, with the same betting signals:

—1 to 8 nickels ($5 to $40), for practice sessions.
—1 to 8 quarters ($25 to $200), our initial betting levels.
—1 to 8 blacks ($100 to $800), when we really got going.

We'd break-in new players at the nickel level. When everything became smooth and the kinks were worked out, we'd progress to greens.

Finally, if and as we started winning, we'd graduate to black chips.

*Playing Signals*

Our brand new playing signals would be:

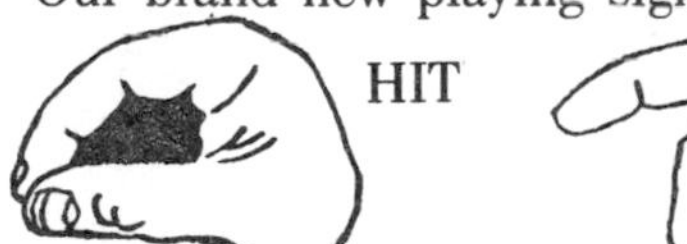


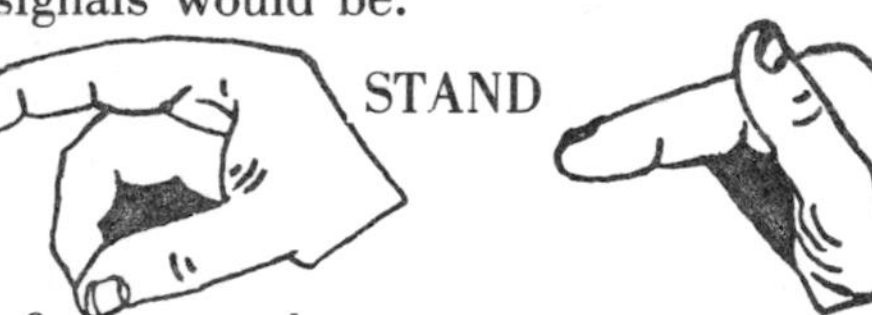


DOUBLE DOWN OR SPLIT

—Hit: thumb and index finger together.
—Stand: thumb and index finger apart.
—Double or Split: thumb raised.

We needed only one signal for doubling and splitting pairs. This was because the BP was instructed: "When you get the thumb-raised signal, if you have a pair, always split them, unless the pair is 4, 4 or 5, 5. Then double down. All other times, double down."*

The only other information the BP needed was whether to take insurance. We used an "audible," for this. If the BP was to take insurance, the counter said, "No."

Otherwise, the counter didn't say a word. Thus, the instant the BP heard "No," he shoved out his insurance bet. If there was silence, the BP didn't take insurance.

## Training

Inga was the dealer. Robert, the BP, sat at third base. We told him to pick his cards up with his left hand and hold them with a natural cant towards the right, so they'd be clearly distinguishable to Bob.

Bob, with his computer, sat in the middle of the table. I sat at first base as a "civilian"—a non-team player—to make the training session more realistic.

The session went horribly. Bob kept giving the wrong signals. He couldn't see Robert's cards. Robert couldn't "read" Bob's signals.

Worst of all, Bob was making errors in reciting the denominations of the unplayed cards. So we knew he was giving his computer the wrong information.

I began to doubt that Bob could get it together. After four hours, we took a lunch break.

Over lunch, we tried to analyze what was going wrong. Bob couldn't get the hit-stand signals right—he'd keep reversing them.

Robert suggested, "Think of your thumb and forefinger together as 'hitting' each other. When they're separated, they're just resting or 'standing' on the table."

Bob was having trouble reading Robert's cards. I told Robert to be

*The one exception to this was when we were playing in a club that allows doubling down after splitting a pair, or "double-after-splits," as we called it. To take an example, if the player drew 9, 9, split them, and drew a 2 on the first 9, he would be able to double down on his total of 11.

When a club allows double-after-splits, the BP splits 4, 4, rather than doubling down.

sure to hold his cards vertically, not sideways, so Bob could more easily read the "index."*

Robert kept putting his bet where Bob did. For example, if Bob signaled a 3 unit bet by putting his chips at the bottom of the betting square, Robert would also put his chips at the bottom of his betting square. It took Robert a while to drop this potentially heat-drawing habit.

We went back to work. After another three hours, Robert was more than ready to play (it doesn't take long to train a BP).

Bob was gradually improving, but still making far too many errors to play in a casino. Once, after a tableful of paint (tens and picture cards) and aces came out on the first round, Bob signaled a bet of 6 chips.

Computer or not, it was obvious that something was wrong.

Bob said, "It might be weak batteries."

Bob changed batteries and we started all over again.

Frank showed up and relieved Robert as BP. Frank was a quick study. In an hour, he was reading the signals with no difficulty.

We were all tired. We quit and arranged to practice some more the following day. Now we had only seven days left of computer play. It didn't look good.

More bad news. The next morning, Tony arrived in town. He looked a lot younger than I'd hoped (young players often draw heat as counters). He also looked like a hood; he wore one of those shirts with the sleeves cut off to the armpits and had a South Philly pompadour haircut.

Although he was only 21, Tony had been married five years. His pregnant wife and two children lived with Tony's mother back in South Philly.

After I got him situated in the condo, he counted down some decks. He was fast, but he was also inaccurate, which I attributed to nervousness. Before long, he improved.

I dealt some hands to him. What a rude shock. Tony had never played a face-down game in his life! In Atlantic City (AC), all the cards are dealt face up. The player is not allowed to touch the cards. In Vegas, the cards are almost universally dealt face down in the

*The "index" is the number or letter written in the upper left-hand corner or lower right-hand corner of a playing card.

single and double-deck games that I was planning on playing, and the player picks his cards up.

There's a big difference, both in playing and in counting cards. In Atlantic City, when the player wants to stand, he moves his hand laterally, to indicate "No more cards." In Vegas, the player tucks the cards under his bet.

When the New Jersey player wants a hit, he scratches the green felt with his fingers. In Nevada, the player scratches the felt with his cards.

In Atlantic City, when the player wants to split or double down, he says it verbally, never touching his cards.

In Nevada, the player throws his cards over, face up, to double down; and turns his cards over, face up and apart, to indicate a pair split.

Tony didn't know the conventions that the most novice of Nevada players knew. This was unnerving, to say the least.

Tony's card-counting problem was even worse. In AC, the counter counts cards after the round is dealt by visually sweeping over all the cards, nicely laid out face up on the table. In Nevada, the player counts cards as they're exposed. Thus if the players to the counter's right stand, those cards remain unexposed, and the counter waits until after the dealer turns those cards up to include them in his count.

The counting techniques between the two states are quite different. I tried to teach Tony the Nevada way.

I dealt Tony a few rounds, cards face down. Tony's count and number of aces was totally screwed up. He didn't have the foggiest idea of how to keep track of the cards when they were dealt face down.

As our session progressed, it became obvious that Tony was not a quick learner. In getting skillful at blackjack, he had had to practice for hours and hours to get even the most rudimentary concept down. He worked long 10 and 12-hour sessions, day after day. Through sheer persistence he had learned the count and the matrix numbers. But there were a few other vital things he didn't know, as I was to find out.

Then Bob came over. I left Tony so I could practice with Bob and his computer.

More errors, or perhaps "weak batteries."

At this point, I was seriously considering returning to San Francisco and forgetting about this new team idea.

It looked as if our "money-making machine" consisted of an unusable computer, an inexperienced Jersey player, and a long-retired, oft-recognized player who might not get any play, even in disguise.

More practice, well into the night. Finally Bob's accuracy with David, while not perfect, seemed good enough for a casino test.

## The First Debacle

I scheduled the very first "David" play for the Stardust. I'd heard through the grapevine that the "Star" had a good single-deck game. I decided to go, too, to get the team "down" and to make sure things went smoothly on our first play.

I always pick "back-up" clubs in case the first club is unplayable (for such reasons as bad conditions or heat on the counter or BP). For this play, I picked the Royal Las Vegas and Westward Ho, both $200-max, single-deck clubs, as the #1 and #2 back-up clubs.

As soon as I walked in the door of the Stardust, I realized I'd made a bad choice. Not only did this club have double-deck, not single-deck, but the penetration was terrible. The dealers were dealing about one deck (half of the pack) and shuffling.

I waited for Bob and Robert, to give them the "ear signal," meaning to go to the back-up club. I never saw them. I assumed that they, too, saw the double-deck games and went to the first back-up club, the Royal Las Vegas.

I couldn't find them at the Royal. Off to the Westward Ho. No luck.

I returned to the Jockey Club and practiced for three hours, wondering what had happened.

Then I heard the team knock—two raps, a pause, and a single rap. In the hallway, I heard Robert, talking in loud tones. (This is usually a good sign. After a win, there's exuberance; after a loss, silence.)

"Ken, we couldn't find you, so we just played it anyway."

"Where'd you play?"

"Why, the Stardust, like we planned."

"But it's double-deck!"

"We figured we'd play there anyway. We won $1,150."

I was happy about the win, but blanched. The Stardust penetration was terrible. But neither Bob nor Robert had even noticed.

Bob and Robert had "played lucky" and won over a grand, even though the conditions were unacceptable.

Then Bob started in on Robert.

"How can you play when you drink so much? You missed a 'chunk' bet (two chips at 12 o'clock). Twice, you missed insurance."

Robert replied, "I never heard you say 'No.'"

Then it was Robert's turn. "You were too slow with the bet signals. I thought the bosses were going to throw me out. I can't sit there with my thumb up my nose, waiting for your signal. It doesn't look right."

The bickering kept up. It was unnerving. What concerned me most was that neither of them had the smarts to know the Stardust game was no good.

I felt Bob over-reacted to Robert's drinking. Bob was a teetotaler; Robert, the last thing from it.

I explained to Bob (and the other counters) that our BP's are permitted, indeed encouraged, to drink. They can booze it up as much as they want, so long as they don't make any mistakes. Rambo once had over 20 drinks over the course of an all-night eight-hour session, had gotten totally smashed, "played" flawlessly—and as a result was loved by the bosses.

Many BP's seem on edge until a few drinks loosen them up. Then, relaxed, more aggressive, and better able to "act," they more naturally go for more audacious betting ratios, which increases the team win rate.

Bob had a very soft voice. Half the time, I had to say "What?" or "Say Again" when he said something in the quietness of our condo. It made sense that Robert could have missed Bob's quiet "No's" amidst the din of the casinos.

I suggested that Bob give the insurance signal more loudly. He didn't take kindly to this criticism.

OK, we'll take the money. But we had a lot of work ahead of us.

The next day, I worked with Tony some more. He was getting totally confused in trying to count the cards as they were dealt face down. To avoid wasting my time dealing to him, and to give him live casino experience, I told him, "Go to one of the single-deck clubs on our list. Play the table for a few hours, until you're comfortable playing the Vegas game. But don't forget, just play the table minimum. You're out to practice, not make money."

Tony had his twelve grand with him. I said, "Just cash in one of the $100 bills, and play a couple bucks a hand."

Tony walked out the door.

Bob, Robert and I dealt a few more hands. I hand-picked some complicated split and re-split pair hands, and a lot of insurance calls. Then I gave Robert $5,000, and sent them off to play the single-deck game at the Marina.

Now it was my time to practice.

I'd been spending my spare time training intensely. I personally practiced by putting together what I called a "Plus 24 deck," a special deck with extra 4's, 5's, 7's and 9's and 8 aces—to make it more difficult to "count it down." It was like swinging two baseball bats, instead of one, in the on-deck circle.

I also made up flash cards to learn the 140 "numbers" that had to be memorized. Each number pertained to a particular "play." For example; if I saw 10 vs. 10 on the card, I recited, "Six."

This meant that if I held 10 versus a dealer 10, I should double down if the count was plus 6 or higher. Otherwise, I would hit the hand.

| 10 |
|---|
| +6 |
| 10 |

So far, I'd been able to practice only about 20 hours. I was far from ready. The count and the "numbers" were coming fine, but I was having a lot of problems with what we call "ace adjustment."

When I learned blackjack, I started with a count called the "Revere 14 Count," then the most powerful system available. The 14 Count required the player to count the number of aces played and to compare this with how many aces normally would have been played if an average number of aces had been dealt.

For example, if one deck out of a four-deck shoe had been dealt, on average, four aces should have been played for aces to be "normal." If six aces were played, the remaining pack was "two aces poor" (six minus four), which is bad for the player. If, say, one ace had been dealt, the pack would be "three aces rich" (four minus one), which benefits the player.

I had to keep track of ace "richness" or "poorness" to adjust the size of the bets.

The difficulty in re-learning ace adjustment was particularly frustrating, because in recent years newer counts had come out that were as powerful as the one I used and which did not require this rigorous exercise.

Further, blackjack expert Arnold Snyder had conducted computer analyses which revealed that, with a system such as the 14 Count, ace adjustment was worth a measley 8 points out of 100 in betting efficiency, if done perfectly.*

So 80% of my training was being spent, impractically, to improve my betting efficiency by a miniscule amount.

Tony also used a count that required ace adjustment, ironically a count I'd developed, called the Uston Advanced Point Count (APC).

The big revelation for me was that the counts that our teams used in the past are far from the best today. It's not the technology—properly applied, the 14 Count and Uston APC are as strong as any system; the problem is that they are too complicated for the average—indeed, above-average—person to learn.

For example, the 14 Count required me to add +4 to the count each time a 5 was played, and a +3 each time a 4 was played. Working with these large numbers contributes to errors. Using a complex system also costs the counter money because he gets tired and cannot play as long; thus his earning potential is reduced.

In addition, with the 14 Count and Uston APC, the player must adjust for aces before making *each* and *every* bet. This is a lot of needless work.**

The very first of the "powerful" systems was Hi Opt 1, developed by Canadian Lance Humble, in the early 1970's. He sold it to players for $100, and thousands used the system, although very few actually paid for it because it was so easily copied on a Xerox.

Then came the 14 Count and Hi Opt 2. Both these counts improved over Hi Opt 1, but still required a separate count of aces. When my

*Furthermore, it was virtually impossible for a player to adjust perfectly for aces, as Snyder's computer runs assumed. Most players adjust to the nearest ace or two aces (estimating the number of cards to be played to the nearest ¼ or ½ deck).

**The older advanced systems did not include aces in the count; they have a zero value. The newer systems, however, assign a minus value to aces. Thus, aces are automatically reflected, for betting purposes, and the adjustment is perfect.

Theoretically, to play the hands perfectly, the player using the newer counts must adjust for aces "in reverse" before playing his hand, but the need to do this occurs in a far fewer percentage of the hands.

mentor, Al Francesco, started his team, the highest powered system available was the 14 Count.

Since that time, I'd developed a system, called the Uston Advanced Plus/Minus, which did not require ace adjustment. I erroneously suggested to readers, in my *Million Dollar Blackjack* that this system was inferior to the Uston APC.

I no longer feel that way. Because of the complexity of the Uston APC and the need to adjust for aces in betting, I now believe the Advanced Plus/Minus to be a far more practical count.

This does not imply that the Uston Advanced Plus/Minus is the only effective system. In fact, one of the best today is Arnold Snyder's Zen Count, which assigns a minus value to aces and does not require ace adjustment for betting purposes.*

These are the types of counts I now recommend when teaching students.

At any rate, rather than having to learn a new count, to say nothing of 140 new index numbers, I continued to practice the 14 Count, working for hours and hours on the tedious ace adjustments required to bet properly.

The team knock interrupted my training. It was Robert. BP's always come back first, since counters are instructed to stay at the table for 15 minutes after the BP has quit. We didn't want the two players leaving together. Also, after the BP's leave, pit bosses often discuss the BP. Overhearing these remarks can be helpful—we'd discover whether the BP was "cool" or not—and we could sometimes make appropriate adjustments to get him better accepted in that club.

Robert said, "My God, we got creamed! I couldn't believe it! Every time I had a 20, the dealer drew a 21. Every time I had a big bet out and doubled down, I'd lose. Whenever I got a blackjack, she had one, too. I lost every insurance bet. It was absurd."

"How much?"

Robert reached in his pocket and pulled out a pathetically thin pack of hundred-dollar bills. He counted them.

"Twelve hundred left. We lost $3,800."

"Any heat on the play?"

*I would subsequently develop an even stronger and simpler count, which is called Uston SS, with which some of our potential teammates would start practicing.

"No. In fact, there was this guy sitting next to me. He lost his shirt—somewhere between five to eight thou. They were watching him, not me."

"It was weird. The guy started betting small, I sort of goaded him on. You know, I'd put out a big bet, saying something like 'Hey, buddy. Why don't you bet something, too?'

"He started playing green chips for a while. Then he pulled out a wad that would choke a cow and started throwing hundred dollar bills around."

Bob walked in the door, with a dour look on his face.

"Robert, damn it! You look at me too obviously. You put heat on me. Use peripheral vision. Don't stare directly at my signals."

I kept repeating, "Every mistake should be a lesson."

We talked until dawn, going over the details of the session and trying to smooth out what we had done wrong.

When I woke up the next "morning" (four P.M.), Tony still hadn't come back. Inga and I were worried about this 21-year-old kid, in Vegas for the first time, with twelve grand in his pocket.

Just after five P.M., Tony finally called.

"Ken, I don't know how to tell you this . . ." Then he paused.

"Where are you?"

"I'm at the Marina. I lost my twelve grand last night."

"What! You were supposed to play dollars."

"I know. But the game was so good, I never seen nuthin' like this single deck. I couldn't believe it. I started bettin' big. I lost five grand. Then I played the four-deck shoe. Came back all the way. Then the cards turned and I lost twelve grand.

"They gave me a suite. I'm comped here."

Never in all of my experience with teams had anyone so crassly violated team rules. I wondered if Tony could really be a counter—or if he was really just a gambler at heart.

I said, "The 12 grand is your loss, not the team's."

"I know."

Our so-called blackjack "team" was down over $2,000—plus $3,000 in expenses.

And I wasn't sure we had a team.

# 9

# The Last Legal Computer Plays

Yes, you guessed it. The crazy high-roller that Robert ran into at the Marina was Tony.

This is terrific. We've got teammates playing at the same table, without knowing each other.

Another comedy of errors.

Neil arrived in Vegas from San Francisco,. The entire team was now in town. We had plenty of BP's. Our problem was Counter Power. I put out the word I was looking for counters.

I called a meeting of the entire team, so everyone could meet each other, and we could review the ground rules for the operation.

There were eight of us gathered in the condo—Bob, Tony and myself, the counters. The BP's were Robert, Neil, Rambo, Frank, and Inga. I went over a list of team rules, which read as follows:

*BP's*

• Come Out in $500's (that is, the BP's should cash in, in increments of $500, so counters can keep track of the money, and be better able to "audit" how much the BP's won or lost).

• Stack Up Chips Neatly at End of Play—and Color Up (cash in red and green chips for black ones). (Also for audit purposes, since the formula was: Chips At End of Play – Dollars Cashed In = Win, or Loss.)

• Bet Exact Amount Signaled by Counter, Plus or Minus $25. (I wanted the counters to determine bet size. I didn't want BP's to vary from the amount signalled for "cover" purposes. In the past, some BP's minimized their bet ratio, or bet more off the top, or didn't "bet it up" when given a "chunk" signal. This keeps the heat off the BP and lengthens his playing life. But it reduces the team's earning power.)

• Come to Jockey Club Before Play, and Right After the Play. (To prevent BP's running around town, or going home, with thousands of team money in their pockets.)

• Sit So You're Naturally Looking in Counter's Direction. (Thus, when looking for signals, the BP's eyes are already directed toward the counter.)

• Scan Counter's Signals, Use Peripheral Vision.

• Don't Go into Your Pockets During the Play, Other Than to Pull Out Cash. (An audit control. It's not hard for a dishonest BP to cop one black chip per session—the very same problem the casinos continually cope with in their employees.)

*Counters*

• Only Team Play Authorized—No Individual Play. (Counters can be tempted to go out and play on their own. This detracts from the reason we're in town—to double the team bank. This rule also avoids such rationalizations as, "Well, I lost $400 while counting for the team, but won it back, playing on my own. So the team owes me $400; but I keep the $400 that I won individually.")

• Rest Before Each Play, Even If Only for 10 Minutes.

• Check the Bad Dealer List Before Each Play. (I'd posted on the wall a list of dealers who gave bad penetration, or who shuffled up when big bets were put out.)

• Remember Bad Dealers, and Add Them to the List.

• Do Not Waste Time on Poor Games. (It's tempting to "get down" and not move to another table or another club, wishfully thinking the dealer will improve, or a better dealer will come in—or simply out of indolence. Playing unprofitable games constitutes one of the principal reasons that counters lose and leave the business.)

In my "straight" years, as Senior Vice President of the Pacific Stock Exchange.

Many years ago, with my idol, Erroll Garner.

My San Francisco "retreat."

Recovering after a run-in with a Pontiac in front of Resorts, February 1979.

Making an instructional blackjack cassette.

Relaxing at the Jockey Club between assaults on the casinos.

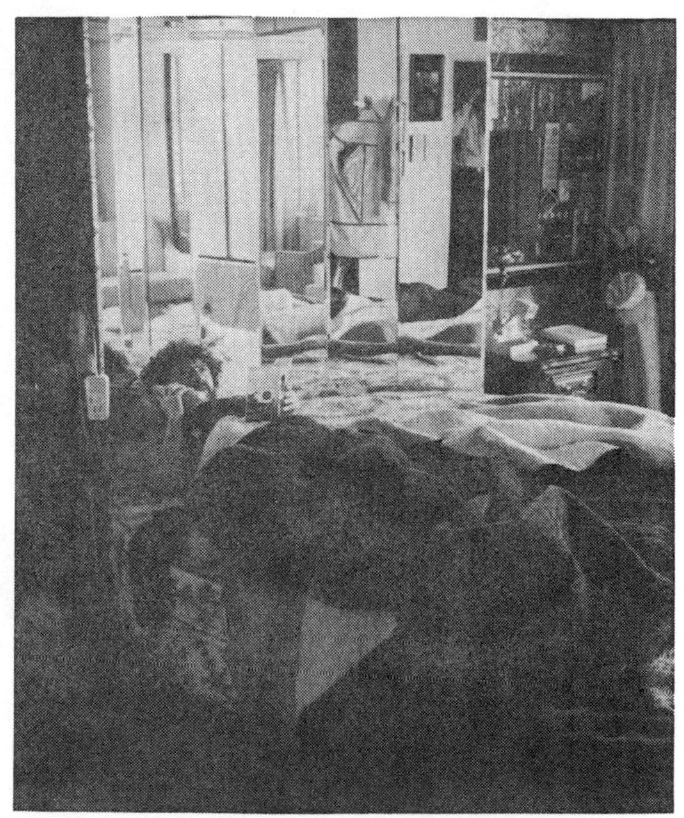

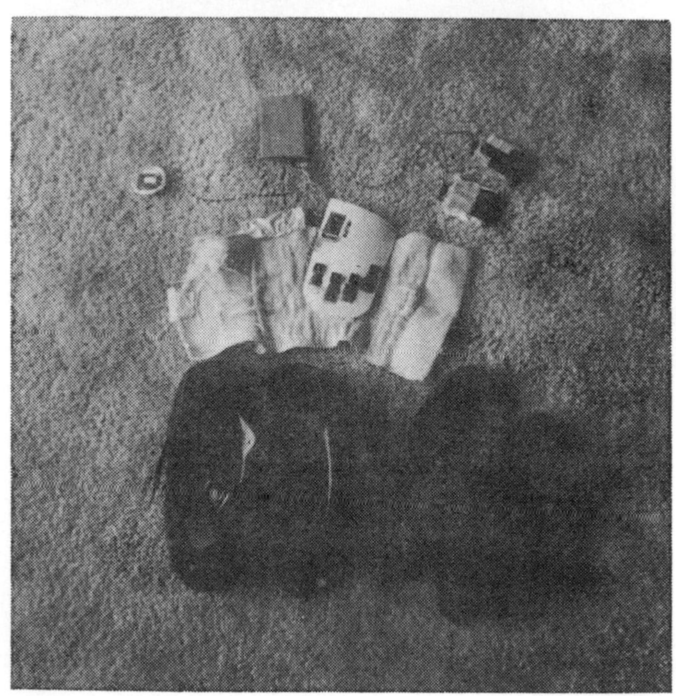

The last computer to play legally in Las Vegas.

Teaching teammates.

One of my better disguises.

Inga and I are comped in Vegas.

After a win at Harrah's Tahoe.

Playing at the Desert Inn.

Comped at Harrah's Tahoe.

Relaxing by playing some jazz in the Jockey Club's lounge.

• Stay at Table at Least 15 Minutes After BP Quits, Listen, and Report Back What You Hear About the BP.

• Don't Stare at the BP's Cards.

*Team*

• Prompt—Be There Right on Time, or Early.

• Random Polygraphs.

• Separate Pockets; If in Doubt, Round in Favor of Team. (Teammates should keep personal money in one pocket, bank money in a separate pocket. Thus there's no "confusion.")

*Signals*

—"BP, sit down" (Hand on cheek).

—"BP, take a break" (Fingers clasped together).

—"There's heat" (Rub forehead with back of wrist).

—"Go to back-up club" (Touch opposite shoulder).

—"End-of-session" (Rub chest).

—"Follow me" (Touch ear).

—"Meet me in men's room" (Touch crotch—not an elegant signal, but it worked).

These signals, of course, allowed us to furtively communicate with each other in the casino.

*Team Knock*

—Two raps; a pause; a single rap. (Just in case some stranger decided to raid my condo, which often had $30,000 or more sitting on a table.)

These controls may seem cold and distrusting, but we'd encountered dishonesty in the past. And honest teammates, of course, would not mind their being imposed.

I've heard numerous horror stories of teams going broke because teammates stole huge amounts from the bank. On Al's first team, one player stole over $60,000 over a year's time. After each session, he'd mail a few hundred dollar bills to himself, in self-addressed envelopes. At 10 to 15 sessions per week, the money added up fast.

At the end of the meeting, Bob collared me with more complaints about Robert. There were only six more days of computer play, and the team was in the hole over $5,000, including expenses.

I decided to conduct a little experiment. I'd be a BP for Bob. Thus I'd be able to check out his computer play. I'd also see if his complaints about Robert were real or imagined, since I'd be Bob's BP myself.

I'd put on a drunken act, and get much higher betting ratios than Robert would. After the play, we'd determine whether there was more money to be made by having me as the BP until the June 30 deadline, or if, instead, I should concentrate on practicing taking out BP's myself as a counter.

For the trial, we would play the single-deck game at the Holiday Riverboat on the Strip.

The BP and pit boss are engaged in a continual cat-and-mouse game, because they have conflicting objectives.

The pit boss is continually watching out for counters or cheats—and also for "legitimate" high rollers whom he can cater to and perhaps win from.

The BP looks for good betting ratios, deep penetration in the deck, and wants to avoid being detected as a counter and barred.

Drawing from the play at the Holiday, let's see how the BP-Boss scenario typically goes.

BP walks into the casino five minutes after the counter, so the counter can "get down" at a table where the dealer's giving good penetration and where there's an open spot to the left of the counter.*

BP sees the counter playing. "Ah. Bob is down at a table with one other player. Perfect."

Now to get established as a harmless "money player."

BP walks up to the table, takes out five $100 bills and says, "Chips, please." BP waits for boss to turn around.

Boss, hearing "Change 500," approaches the table. "What do we have here? High-roller? Counter? Cheat? Nut?"

BP peripherally spots boss's glance. BP slurs to dealer, as if boss didn't exist, "Lemme havva vodka grape. Could ja make it a double?"

Boss: "The guy's drunk. Betting some money. So far, so good."

*It's preferable for the BP to be to the left of the counter. This allows the counter to get rid of his cards prior to using his hand to signal the BP how to play.

BP gets chips. Stares "blankly" around. His eyes are "attracted" by a keno board in front of the table. BP thinks, "This is perfect."

BP spots boss "for first time." BP smiles at Boss, saying, "Can I play keno, too?"

Boss said, "Sure," thinking, "It looks like this guy's a gambler."

BP says, "What's the top pay-off? Twelve-five? Twenty-five grand?"

Boss doesn't know the answer and says, "I'll find out for you." Boss thinks, "He looks like a real gambler. Let's make him happy and keep him here."

Boss goes to podium, finds a keno betting schedule, and gives it to BP.

BP takes the keno schedule. Says, "Twenty-five grand if I get 8 numbers out of 8!" BP quickly glances at Bob's betting signal (it's for a small bet—$100), and carelessly throws out three green chips. Adds one red for the dealer. "This is for you, honey. Let's make some money." An apparent afterthought (he's used that line before), "Hey! That rhymes!"

BP suspects that the dealer's thinking, "What a macho asshole." BP's intent is to be viewed as exactly that.

BP says to Boss, "Can I have a keno girl?"

Boss walks off to summon a keno girl.

BP plays without anyone watching him for three or four minutes. Boss comes back to the table. Now it's time to assess this guy's play.

Dealer shuffles. BP was betting a stack of seven greens. BP recklessly shovels in the greens into a random pile of chips of all colors in front of him. BP throws a black on the betting square.

Dealer starts dealing. BP yells, "Wait a minute," and throws another black on top.

Boss thinks, "Great. He bets big after the shuffle. He makes impulsive bets. He's drunk. He plays keno. He's ours."

Boss relaxes.

BP loses. BP laughs and shrugs the loss off with, "You gotta run with the big dogs, you gotta shit with 'em too."

Dealer doesn't even flinch at the profanity. Boss laughs. So does Bob.

BP sees Bob signaling a "chunk" bet.

BP throws out three hundred-dollar bills on betting square, ignoring the chips piled in front of him. BP sees boss watching, and immediately, and loudly, orders another drink, almost "falling off" his stool.

Boss claps for a cocktail waitress. There's none to be had. Boss goes over to waitress station to summon a cocktail waitress. Then boss runs to the podium to make three marks on a pad, recording the BP's $300 "drop."

BP, now unwatched, bets more aggressively, both up and down, in accordance with Bob's betting signals.

Boss returns. BP has 16 versus 10. (Bob signals "Stand"). Dealer is waiting for BP to play his hand. But, despite his $400 bet, BP has "lost interest" in his hand and is preoccupied with the numbers popping up on the keno board.

BP slurs, "Let's see, this is game #356. I got three numbers so far!"

BP suddenly "notices" it's his turn to play. With a shrug, BP says, "Naw. Don't hit it," and quickly looks back at the keno board.

BP wins $400, but hardly notices. Dealer shuffles.

BP impulsively pulls back his eight chips into his mass of silver, red, green and black chips sloppily piled in front of him.

BP glances quickly across the pit. Boss is watching, thinking, "What's he going to do off the top?"

BP slurs, "OK. 'S time for a rainbow bet."

BP picks up a black, green, red, and silver and stacks them on the betting square. Then, as an afterthought, he grabs a 50-cent piece and puts it on top.

Bosses like this crazy betting, not even thinking that the BP has lowered his bet from $400 to $131.50.

BP wins. BP conspicuously ignores all the other players' cards, as the dealer turns them up.

Boss notices this. "This guy's no counter—no way."

Bob has two chips at 12 o'clock, the signal for a "chunk" bet.

BP says, "OK. Time for the double rainbow." BP stacks up the chips on the square—two blacks, two greens, two reds, two silvers, and two 50-cent pieces. BP "miscounts" and happens to slide a third black chip under the stack. The BP's now betting almost $400 again ($363). No one seems to notice or care.

Boss sees the absurd-looking bet, and notices that BP is slurring more loudly. "OK. No problem. We could really take this guy for some money."

Boss relaxes and walks away.

BP notices the boss leaving. He knows he's "in."

A good-looking girl, braless, in a tight T-shirt (it's 110 degrees in Vegas) sits down at BP's left. BP looks at girl, "Hey. Howya doin'?"

Girl smiles back. Hooker-type. Huge chest.

BP says, "Let's win some money for you," and throws a $5 chip on the girl's stack.

Girl smiles.

Boss smiles.

BP smiles.

BP now has about $2,500 in chips piled in front of him. No one can tell exactly. The first boss is not even watching the game. A second boss comes over to the table.

BP spots the second boss, peripherally. Just as the second boss gets to the table, BP orders a double, again "drunkenly" slips off his chair, and regains his balance. Then the BP gets totally "distracted" from the game by a passing buxom waitress, just as the dealer exposes the players' cards, none of which the BP notices.

Second boss takes all this in.

BP wins a $300 bet. Bob signals "chunk." BP has $600 in front of him. BP "slops" the six black chips into the betting square.

"Let it ride."

Dealer says, "Sorry, sir. The limit's $500."

BP says, "Oh. Thanks. You probably saved me money." He doesn't touch the chips, saying, "If I lose, just take what you need."

Dealer turns to the second boss.

Boss nods and says, "Chips play to the limit."

Boss smiles.

BP wins. Dealer shuffles.

BP starts flirting with the girl on his left, ignoring the new deal.

Dealer says, "Bet, sir?"

BP grabs a handful of red and green chips and, not even looking, throws them in the direction of the betting square, as he continues to flirt with the girl.

The dealer arranges the mass of chips into a stack (the stack is tall, but worth only about $125).

Eventually everyone at the table, as well as the dealer, the two pit bosses, and Bob, are laughing and enjoying the reckless, eccentric high-roller.

After a few hours, Bob gives the "end of session" signal.

BP gathers in his chips, throws a green one to the dealer, and staggers to the cashier's cage.

First boss quickly runs after him, handing the BP his business card, saying, "Call me, if you ever want anything here."

Bob returns to the condo. Both he and I agree that there's far more money to be made with plays like this one. The betting ratios are far more extreme. I decided to be a BP until the computer became illegal in five days.

Bob and I repeated our little act at Circus Circus, the Westward Ho, and the Dunes.

Bob also took out Inga and Rambo. I kept him away from Robert.

Bob's last computer play was also at the Holiday Riverboat—on the evening of June 30. Rambo was the BP.

Bob was sitting in the middle of the table. Rambo was at third base (the extreme left seat). A man in a business suit came up behind them and started watching the game. Bob thought he saw the man looking at his feet. After ten minutes of this, Bob became too unnerved to play. He was convinced that the spectator was an agent from Griffin Investigations, the private detective agency that patrols casinos looking for counters, computer players, and cheats.

Bob was afraid of getting busted and being detained in a back room until after the midnight deadline, thus risking a minimum of one year in jail. He wisely called off the play.

Rambo, Bob and "David" won $300, on what was one of the last, if not the very last, legal computer blackjack plays in the state of Nevada.

We had hoped to win $30,000 or more in the final days with David. Because of delays and training problems, we played far fewer hours than we'd hoped. But Bob and David did win around $8,000 for the team.

Now it was time to play blackjack cerebrally, rather than electronically.

A final reminder: if you're tempted, as you read this, to run the risk of using this little money-making gadget, remember the penalty is right up there with robbing a bank.

And to rob a bank, you need a lot less starting capital.

# 10

# Back in Action

Tony, Bob and I were all practicing frenetically. Tony, painfully aware of his $12,000 personal loss from his little escapade at the Marina, was anxious to make that money back—plus some. He was down to his last $10,000, and his wife, back in South Philly, was expecting their third child. Nevertheless, Tony hung in and instructed his wife to wire him $8,000, which he put into the team bank.

Bob couldn't play with David anymore and flew back to Irvine, California, to get his master's in mathematics. The timing, for him, was perfect; his school semester was scheduled to begin in one week.

I recruited three more counters. Allen had played with me on an earlier team and was highly experienced. He drove in from Los Angeles and was ready to play two days later.

A second counter, Rollie, had been winning in Vegas, and although he used a weaker count (a plus-1/minus-1 count that Tony disparagingly referred to as a "Gay Count"), he seemed good enough to play for us. The third player to join us, Glynn, used the 14 Count. Glynn had been playing for ten years, and had personally won well into six figures.

I had two trainees in the Bay Area. Both were working with the so-called Uston SS count.

The team was gradually getting tighter. After another week of practice, Tony was finally able to count the face-down game accurately.

When I felt ready to play, I went out and got a short haircut; it was almost a crewcut. Then I shaved off my beard and moustache. It's weird when you see your chin for the first time in ten years.

I decided to start small, at a $200-maximum club, Joe Slyman's Royal Las Vegas. The Royal single-deck game has Strip rules, so the player is dead even off the top. Inga would be the BP.

I took $5,000 out of the safety deposit box that we'd had installed in my Jockey Club condo. I put on a baseball hat and a pair of fake prescription glasses.

When our cab reached the Royal, Inga and I went in through separate entrances. The Royal was crowded (it was Saturday) and there were three bosses watching the games—two in the blackjack pit, one standing over the craps table. None of them looked familiar. The owner, Joe Slyman, who'd known me years ago and had even said "Hello" to me (when I was in full beard, moustache, and long, curly hair) at the Commission hearing only two weeks before was nowhere to be seen.

A player in a cowboy hat was betting $200 a hand at one of the single-deck games. (Other high-rollers at the table often divert the bosses' attention and take the "heat" off our players.)

I slid into a seat to the right of the cowboy, and observed the game. Betting $5 a hand. The dealer was going real deep into the deck. I put my hand on my cheek. Inga, across the pit, spotted the signal and walked around the pit toward the table. She sat down, to the left of the cowboy, who had about $3,000 in black chips in front of him. Inga put five one-hundred-dollar bills on the table.

The dealer turned toward the boss.

"Changing five hundred."

The boss glanced at Inga and nodded, "Go ahead."

I put my bet at 12 o'clock on the betting square. Inga put out four green chips.

The cowboy said, "Good luck, honey," and put out a $200 bet.

The dealer had a nine showing. The cowboy hit a pair of eights and drew a five (he made the wrong play, but drew the right cards).

Inga had a 7 and 4.

I tucked my 17 and rested my hand on the table, raising my thumb slightly.

Inga glanced over, slid out 4 more green chips, and said, "Double."

The dealer had a six in the hole, and drew a seven, busting. The dealer paid Inga, with two black chips.

The count had gone up. I put two nickels at 12 o'clock, which signaled a "chunk" bet. Inga left the two black chips on the betting square.

She drew a 13. I put my finger and thumb together, and Inga drew a card and busted. Now we were even again.

We played on for two hours. The bosses, wary at first of this young female high-roller, gradually accepted Inga's action. They were far more interested in the cowboy, who had lost $3,000 while we'd been playing with him.

Then Joe Slyman walked into the casino from the hotel reception area. He conferred softly with the boss who was watching our game. He glanced at the cowboy and at Inga.

My heart began to pound, and my hands started shaking. I continued to give signals to Inga, but held my head down so Joe couldn't see my eyes.

I could tell Joe was looking at all the players at the table. Finally he walked away.

The disguise had worked! If Joe hadn't recognized me, it wasn't likely that many other bosses would.

A few days later, I took Robert to the Trop. I put on the baseball cap and the fake prescription glasses. Before entering the casino, I pushed the cap down the back of my head so it forced my ears to stick out.

The very instant I sat down at the $25 double-deck game, I spotted Jack Newton, a boss whom I had done business with in the past.

Jack had been a counter himself. He later moved to the other side of the table, working the floor at the Horseshoe and then quitting to become Casino Manager of the now defunct Treasury Casino.

Four years ago, the owner of the Treasury, Herb Pastor, had contacted me to discuss a promotional idea he had dreamed up. His plan was to have me teach blackjack in his showroom on weekends, in order to get players for his casino.

Herb launched the project with a news conference and an extensive ad campaign. A *Wall Street Journal* reporter who attended the news conference interviewed other Vegas casino executives to get their reaction to Herb's seemingly heretical plan to teach people how to play winning blackjack.

The owner of the Dunes told the reporter, "No, no, no," a quote that made the front page of the *Journal*. The article ended, "When told of the Dunes' reaction, Pastor responded, 'Yes, yes, yes.'"

During the Treasury project, I'd worked closely with Jack Newton. Together, we'd filmed a blackjack match which was aired as a TV special. Jack and I were in daily contact for months.

Herb's promotion generated a tremendous amount of publicity, but not much business. The reason: at the seminars, I told the players to go home and practice. Apparently they followed this advice, rather than playing in the Treasury's casino. Jack Newton was now standing five feet away from me in the Tropicana casino. He glanced at me. I put on a phony smile, hinging my lower teeth in front of the upper ones, to contort the shape of my face.

Jack smiled at me. I interpreted Jack's expression as a knowing smile that conveyed, "Come on, Kenny. What are you trying to pull off now?"

I was ready to "confess."

To my surprise, Jack quickly looked away. My God! He hadn't recognized me.

I flashed Robert the signal to sit down. He threw $500 on the table. Jack came over and checked Robert out. I put on the phony smile again. Jack didn't even glance in my direction.

Robert and I played four hours. Whenever Jack came over to see how Robert was doing, I'd smile and look down, so my eyes were hidden by the visor of the baseball cap.

Robert won $4,500. One boss "comped" him to a suite. The play had worked.

Our team started encountering some hilarious incidents—and a few infuriating ones.

I found a good game at the Stardust, of all places. I was calling plays, as a counter, for Neil, the BP. For the first hour, the play was fine, but the cards were terrible. Neil "went in" for $3,000. Finally the cards turned. In ten minutes, Neil swung back by $7,000 and was up $4,000.

This brought the shift manager, an old nemesis, Phil DiGardi, to the table. Phil has barred me a dozen times at the Stardust. He checked out Neil. Then his eyes swept across the other players at the table. They focused on me and stopped. I, of course, didn't look back. I could feel Phil staring me down, despite my short hair, baseball cap, and sunglasses.

Phil walked away from the table, and, without looking at me, he yelled, "Kenny," to test my reaction.

I didn't respond.

Phil kept watching me closely. I felt conspicuous trying to give signals to Neil, and rubbed my chest, signaling Neil to quit. Not wanting to quit at the same time as Neil, I kept playing. Phil kept watching me. Finally I grabbed my chips, left the table, and walked away.

Phil followed me. To avoid a confrontation with him, I quickly twisted through the dense crowd and slipped into the men's room. It was empty.

Phil followed me into the john. I jumped into a stall, left the door closed, but unlocked, and raised my feet.

Phil walked from one end of the room to the other, looking under each stall.

He saw nothing and walked out the door.

It's weird how grown men behave in Vegas.

Tony and I went to the Trop to count for Rambo. The "plan": Tony and I would sit at adjacent tables. When the count became favorable, we'd each signal Rambo (hand on cheek) to move to our table. Thus Rambo could jump back and forth between both tables, which would be less likely to put heat on either Tony or me.

Rambo played outrageously-bold ratios, often varying from $25 on one hand to $500 on the next. When he won, he'd let out an animal-like howl, which could be heard throughout the casino. Even the typically raucous craps bettors were looking over at Rambo. When he lost, he'd wildly wave his trunk-like arms in the air.

Although Rambo's King Kong act was convincing, I flinched when he did this, because he'd sometimes come within inches of the dealer. If he happened by accident to connect, he'd knock the poor dealer halfway across the pit.

Rambo was at my table and had lost $1,000 double down. He grunted loudly, waved his arms, and knocked over his Bloody Mary. The table, cards, and chips were soaked with ice, booze, tomato juice, and pieces of lime. The dealer grabbed a towel. A boss ran over with new decks of cards. At that instant, Tony, at the next table, put his hand to his cheek, signaling that his deck was hot.

Rambo, seeing Tony's signal, looked at the mess on the table, grabbed his chips, and walked to Tony's table. As he left, he complained, "I don't play at wet tables."

Tony and I went to the Dunes. The plan: Tony would call plays; I'd be the BP, since I was known as a high-roller at the Dunes, having been a BP with Bob and his computer.

The game was fabulous. Double-deck, dealt face up, and the added player options of surrender and double down on split pairs.

My "name" was Billy Williams. Within an hour, I was stuck $7,000, betting up to $1,000 a hand. The pit liked the action. A yuppie pit boss-ette offered to comp me.

My policy is always to take the comps, whether they're used or not. This puts the boss in your corner. He's now on record as having been convinced that you are a "good" player. Thus, he's made a business judgment, and won't be motivated to look for evidence to prove that he was wrong.

She said, "Let me have your driver's license for the front desk. I'll register you."

I needed a reason to turn the comp down.

"Forget it. I don't want the IRS to know I'm here."

After a long, hard five hours, we came back $7,500, and quit $500 ahead. I put the money in the cage.

The following day, I returned to the Dunes, with Allen as my counter. I went to the cage to pull the money out. The cashier looked at my credit slip and immediately grabbed a telephone, saying,

"Mr. Vickery asked me to call him. One moment, please."

Vic Vickery was the Dunes' brand new Director of Casino Operations. Vic and I had been friendly in the past. In fact, just several months earlier, when he was at the Riviera, Vic organized a dinner to be hosted by several well-known names in blackjack. Vic had invited me to speak, as well as other blackjack authorities, including Ed Thorpe, Arnold Snyder, and Stanford Wong. The affair never came off because Vic left the Riviera, and his replacement wasn't thrilled with the idea of a dinner for "the enemy."

Vic came over to the cage.

"Kenny, you're my friend. How come you're playing here?"

"Vic, you're my friend, too. But you've got about the best game in town. How'd you expect me to stay away?"

Vic laughed, sort of.

I asked, "How'd you know it was me?"

"Herb Nunez saw you yesterday on the way out the door." Herb, another old nemesis, was now graveyard shift manager at the Dunes. I cursed the luck. I'd hoped to get a lot of play in at the Dunes' candy store.

I told Vic I wouldn't play the Dunes anymore. Of course, that didn't mean that teammates couldn't play there. Later, when I played in disguise, I broke my word to Vic and snuck into the Dunes several times to play. I'm not proud of that.

A few days later, I was back at the Dunes. Now to explain this little caper, you have to understand that I've always felt that when you work at something, it should be fun, too. Or else, why do it?

Bearing that in mind, I'll relate a story—and maybe you'll understand. I'd been out playing with Neil, and had a nice night—up $4,250 at the Sands, and no heat.

I went back to the Jockey Club. All the other guys were still out. But I felt like celebrating. So I went over to the Dunes, where I knew Tony and Frank were playing.

I walked in, unobserved, and saw my players grinding away at a double-deck game in the main pit. Tony was counting and signaling; Frank was betting the big money. I stood away from their table, by a roulette game, keeping out of view of the watching bosses.

I decided that I'd jump in with a $500 bet when the count got good, play one hand, and run. It was mainly for fun, to show Tony and Frank that, even though I'd recently been caught by Vic Vickery, I'd give the Dunes a little tweak. I thought my teammates would get a kick out of it.

First, I left and went to the Dunes gift shop to buy a hat for a disguise. The shop didn't have any hats; the only article usable for my purposes was some garish gag underpants that were tastelessly preprinted, "I crapped out in Vegas" (only in Vegas).

I bought a pair; I needed some kind of disguise.

I put the pants in my pocket, and went back to the casino. After a few minutes, the dealer shuffled, and the count soared to a phenomenal level of +31. The players had an edge of about 4%.

I slid the pants over my head right down to the top of my eyeballs. They fit tightly and looked like a stocking mask. I threw $500 on the betting square next to Frank, and said, "Play it."

When Tony and Frank saw me, they both cracked up.

I was standing at third base, next to a large pole that hid me from most of the pit. As I put out the bet, I noticed my old friend, Herb Nunez, leaning against the pole, but looking at another game. I made sure to stay out of his sight.

I won the hand.

Some perverse notion made me say, "I just flew in from Frisco—my lucky city. Anybody here's name begin with 'F'?" (I knew, of course, that Frank was playing under his real name).

I turned toward Tony and said, "What's your name?"

Tony lied, "Bob."

Frank yelled out, "My name's Frank!"

I said, "OK, it's your lucky day." I tossed him my cash and chips, saying, "These are yours."

Then I slid the pants off my head, and threw them on the table. I said, "All right! I did *NOT* crap out in Vegas," and ran out of the casino.

I later found out that the bosses tried to take the money away from Frank. One boss lied, "Oh, that guy comes in here all the time and does that. We always keep his money for him."

Sure you do, buddy.

Childish of me? Yeah, I know.

I was gradually getting heat around town.

I took Neil to the Westward Ho. I wore the baseball cap. Stupidly, I lowered my head too obviously every time the boss walked by, which, of course, made him suspicious.

Finally the boss reached over and pulled up my visor. Then he nearly ran to the pit stand and grabbed a new deck of cards. He gave it to the dealer. I whispered to Neil, "Get ready. Here it comes."

Within minutes, I felt a tap on my shoulder. Two security guards were standing in back of my chair.

"We'd like a word with you."

"Sure."

"We don't want your action here. Follow me."

They led me out the door and, once outside, read me the Trespass Act:

"If you return to this casino, we can, and will, have you arrested for trespassing."

When Neil finally got back to the condo he told me they'd done the same thing to him.

We couldn't figure out what had happened. When bosses suspect the presence of card-markers or card-muckers (cheats who take cards out of the deck), they suddenly change cards and either count them or examine them.

Did the boss mistake us for a couple of cheats? Did he know it was me? Why did the boss react so quickly when he saw my face? If he knew it was me, a counter, why did he change the deck so suddenly?

We never did figure out what happened.

I walked into the Sahara to call plays for Rambo. I sat down at a $25 double-deck game and made one bet. A real ugly boss, with a pock-marked face, walked by the table and "non-watched" me. (A few years back, bosses tended to stare counters down. Now, I found, many pretended not to be "on" to the counter and tried consciously not to be caught observing the game.)

Off in the distance, Moon Face was talking with three other bosses. I heard the name "Uston," grabbed my chips, and hit the door. Somehow the Sahara always seems to spot me, whether I'm in long hair, short hair, or disguise.

Tony took Inga to Caesars. To fit in with the Caesars crowd, Inga was dressed to the hilt.

They sat down at one of Caesars four four-deck games (all the rest are six decks).

The table was full—four of Caesar's high-rolling regulars, Inga and Tony. Because Inga had no credit line at Caesars, she wasn't a known customer. The bosses, while not "sweating" her action, weren't particularly friendly. Tony, with his armless shirt cut to his hairy armpits, looked decidedly out of place. He flat bet quarters.

Inga's bets varied from $100 to $1,000. The cards ran well for the entire table. The Caesars regulars were cheering, bantering with Inga, and calling her "Lady Luck."

The bosses were giving Tony dirty looks, as if to say, "Who's this scruffy-looking guy, taking up a seat betting a lousy $25 per hand?"

Inga went up to $5,500. Tony gave her the "end-of-session" signal.

When "Lady Luck" quit winners, so did three of the regulars. That didn't particularly please the bosses.

The BP act was working for the team even better then I had hoped. Our BP's were varying from $25 to $500, an enormous 20-to-1 ratio, which was far more than enough to beat the double-deck game. Most bosses didn't even flinch, since the BP's were getting drunk, not looking at the cards, and generally acting like screwballs.

We began getting lots of "hours in." Twice each day I'd send out three or four teams simultaneously. Averaging about 20 hours a day, with an earnings rate of over $300 per hour, our "expected value," as we call it, was about $6,000 per day.

Our earnings started reflecting our advantage. Within a little over a week, we were up over $30,000. I mixed up the BP's and counters, so a given casino shift rarely saw the same faces together at the table.

There are many reasons why playing blackjack for a living is more fun than just about anything else I can imagine:

—You're on your own; there's no one to take orders from; no boss or Board to report to; no three-piece suit to wear.

—You can play any time, day or night; this appeals particularly to people who don't like to get up in the morning. (There is an exception to this—when the alarm rings at four A.M. for graveyard play, I envy the nine-to-fivers who can sleep until seven or eight.)

—The money's usually real good—enough to allow most blackjack players to take lots of time off, to travel, relax, or just bum around.

—There's something about sitting in a casino, betting money, putting on an act, especially on a Monday, when the rest of the world is starting their workweek, commuting on their trains, subways, and buses, and grinding away. I often think of an ex-roommate of mine at college who's been commuting two hours—each way—every day for the past 12 years from his home in Princeton, New Jersey, to his office in Manhattan.

—When blackjack goes good, it goes really good. (When it goes bad, it's horrible.) But, for the moment, let's dwell on the positive. To wit:

After a good session, the counter can walk away ten or fifteen thousand dollars richer—all in cash—and, as many times as not, the bosses love the action, and offer comps to gourmet meals and luxury rooms, and make the player feel like a king.

The counter can ply his trade in most parts of the world. There are beatable games in England, France, Monte Carlo, Korea, the Philippines, the Caribbean, and South America.

The blackjack counter generally has a lot of cash in his pocket. This attracts women—often the wrong type, but so be it. Lots of cash can lead to absurd spending habits—and I freely admit to being one of the worst offenders. But I believe the money's there to be spent—and I do seem to go through an awful lot of it.

Strangely, nearly all the money I spend is for services, not goods. American Express accounts for about half of my spending, and that's nearly all for restaurants, hotels, rental cars, limos, and airfares. I don't own a car (I travel too much to need one) and don't like boats, private planes, or expensive clothes. My weakness: I like to eat at fancy restaurants, and have done so just about every night for the past fifteen years.

Sometimes, though, blackjack can go really bad—as we were about to find out.

# 11

# Appealing the Commission's Decision

Although the team was now up over $30,000, I had to take time out to continue the legal battle. In Nevada, there's a statute (NRS 463.315) which allows a "person aggrieved" by a Commission decision to go to court (it's called "judicial review"). The aggrieved party is given 20 days to file a petition.

It was now Day 18, definitely the eleventh hour.

My heart was not in doing legal research; blackjack playing seemed far more important, more fun, more profitable.

But the team would get along without me. I told Allen to do the team scheduling for the following day, put my phone on "Do Not Disturb," and pulled out the massive legal files.

Before long, I was totally engrossed in this crusade. Each time I read the file about the people who have been forced into back rooms against their will, treated like crooks, arrested, and even beat up, I got a little more dedicated.

I've been arrested once or twice. It's a terrifying experience. If you've ever been handcuffed and locked up in a cell, you know the feeling. And in Nevada they can throw you behind bars just for playing blackjack too well. And that goes on your record.

As I mentioned, I've had bones broken twice—once in Reno, once in Atlantic City.

Another counter, Jonathan Ungar, was also physically accosted. Here's how he described it (in an affidavit we submitted to the Commission):

"On December 31, 1981, I was playing blackjack at the Imperial Palace. A man asked me to cash in my chips and leave. . . . I was detained by a uniformed guard who said that security wanted to ask me some questions.

"I was forcibly taken against my will to a security office where two men were waiting. [A] Mr. Shindell struck me in the face with a closed fist with enough force to knock me down and said that I had a lot to learn about life. A friend of mine (also a counter) was being held in another office.

"I was held in that office for two hours. Throughout the two hours, I was repeatedly threatened, including Mr. Shindell playing with a bolt-cutter and talking about breaking fingers off. They refused my repeated request to call the police. They also threatened to take all of my money if I did not pay them off. Finally I paid them $7,000 and [was] photographed and read the Trespass Act.

"Mr. Shindell then distributed our photographs to a number of casinos describing us as 'suspected card cheats,' although there had never been any suspicion of any wrongdoing. We filed suit and settled in April, 1984."

Despite this horror story, counters were still huge underdogs legally. It didn't make sense.

## The Court Petition

Nevada law says that, in filing a petition for judicial review, one must set forth: "The grounds or reasons why Petitioner contends a reversal or modification should be ordered."

I used all the ammunition I could find, quoting Nevada laws and drawing from the arguments that worked with the New Jersey Supreme Court. The main points put in the petition:

1. The commission was given evidence that counters had been barred, detained and photographed against their will, arrested, and even beat up. Thus their decision condones these undesirable actions.

2. Nevada law spells out who the Commission can have excluded from casinos (and listed in the so-called "Black Book"), citing known felons, tax evaders, and notorious and unsavory persons. Nowhere are counters listed.

3. Even people in the Black Book must be served notice and can appeal their "barring." Yet counters, who break no law, do not have these rights.

4. Nevada law says the games should be run following "proper standards of custom, decorum and decency," and without "reflecting on the repute of the State of Nevada."

How does offering a game of skill, and allowing play to unskillful, compulsive and degenerate gamblers, but arbitrarily throwing out skillful players, be considered in accordance with "proper standards of custom, decorum, and decency"?

5. How can bosses spot counters (most don't count themselves). Counting is a silent, thinking process. The bosses would have to use mental telepathy to know who to throw out.

6. The bosses can use counting as an excuse to throw out anyone they choose. Surely the Legislature didn't intend this.

7. By letting casinos throw out counters, the Commission is encouraging use of the "Mug Book," which has illegal pictures and dossiers of suspected counters, a crass invasion of privacy and violation of our basic rights. The Mug Book is published and circulated by Griffin Investigations, Inc., a private detective agency.

8. The Mug Book also lists casino cheaters and dishonest employees. So counters, who have done nothing illegal, are grouped right in with known criminals.

9. The secret Mug Book is used insidiously. On the first page of the book, is printed:

"No one is to be told that he is in the Mug Book.

"No one is to be asked not to play, or to leave the Casino, using the fact that he is in the Mug Book as a reason for the action.

"No pages or photographs shall be removed from the Mug Book by anyone other than persons authorized by Griffin Investigations or Argy, Inc."

10. Jersey and Nevada gaming law is almost identical—and the Jersey Supreme Court has ruled:

"The Commission alone has authority to exclude patrons based upon strategies for playing licensed casino games; therefore, the Act precluded casino from excluding patron based on his 'card counting' method of playing blackjack . . ."

11. If Nevada adopts no-barring, the casinos can shuffle and take other measures to protect themselves against counters, just as they are doing in New Jersey.

12. The vast majority of public opinion is against barring. This constitutes a violation of Nevada law, which reads that Nevada gaming should promote "public confidence and trust" in licensed gaming.

As a sample of public opinion, I attached copies of editorials from three major U.S. newspapers:

—*The Los Angeles Times,* in an editorial entitled "Vegas Vultures," stated,

"A number of casinos in Las Vegas won't let Kenneth Uston play blackjack at their tables because he's too good at it. . . . In other words he can play 21 only if he loses more often than he wins.

"That bothers us. We have always been taught to try to excel at whatever we do. The casinos, however, regard that as a vice, not a virtue.

"Nothing that Uston was doing was illegal, but what those vultures do is an open-and-shut case of grand larceny. And if there isn't a law against that in Nevada, there out to be."

—*The New York Daily News,* in an editorial entitled "Rubes Only," wrote,

". . . The state should turn thumbs down on the casino ejection [of card-counters] policy. The house has enough of an edge in the odds as it is. Why should players—even pros—be denied a chance to wager just because they have ways to improve their chances?"

—Even the lofty *New York Times* ran an editorial entitled "Loaded Odds," saying,

"In accordance with the principle that an educated consumer is their worst customer, the casinos of Las Vegas bar people who play blackjack so shrewdly that the odds are turned in their favor. Mr. Uston sued. Mr. Uston and his like seem to us to have justice on their side. If the casinos do not admit smart players as well as suckers, where's the gamble?"

I thought my petition was pretty persuasive and was proud of it. Later I found that it was a very poorly prepared legal document.

Robert, an ex-writer, agreed to help me with some of the legal chores. We found a 24-hour Xerox joint—only in Vegas—and ran off what seemed like a thousand sheets of paper ($150 worth) for the courts, the Commission, our files, and the gambling media.

We felt we *had* to inform the media to have any chance at all of getting a fair shake in Nevada. As I said, I believe the *60 Minutes* coverage had a lot to do with our victory in New Jersey.

Up all night, we went to court to file the papers and to the post office to mail off a dozen copies.

Robert and I were chortling, feeling a bit smug and optimistic. We felt we did good work and that now, by statute, the Commission must get to work, preparing rebuttals and compiling hearing transcripts and other material for the court appeal.

Our mood changed after we delivered, by hand, a copy of the petition to the Commission (I had thought it'd be interesting to visit their offices in person).

We gave our petition to a Commission lawyer. He perused it and said, almost immediately:

"Your argument isn't valid because the statutes apply only to persons who were aggrieved because of disciplinary actions."

Off the record, the lawyer went on, "I've read your books," and was kind enough to cite another statute that he thought might have helped us (it didn't), quickly adding, "Don't tell anyone I told you this."

Robert and I went back to the Jockey Club, quite distraught. Our earlier elation was replaced by, "Was all this work for nothing?"

We read and re-read the statutes. It still seemed to us that things were OK, but suspected that a Nevada judge would be likely to interpret things along the lines of the Commission lawyer, rather than agreeing with some out-of-state upstart.

We went out for a drink, and ran into an old friend who, after listening to our story, chilled me with the simple caution:

"Be careful. They never found Jimmy Hoffa."

That night, I saw a TV movie about the Soviet dissident, Andrei Sakharov. At one point, Mrs. Sakharov raised a glass of vodka and said, "A toast – a toast to the success of our hopeless cause."

I sipped my glass of wine and said, "Hear, hear."

# 12

# We Run into a Buzz Saw

Our team goal was to "double the bank." And we were within shooting distance; we'd won $30,000, and had another $20,000-plus to go.

When the bank is doubled, we "break the bank"—that is, calculate how much each teammate has got coming back.

Investors get half of the win, in direct proportion to the amount of their investment.

The other half of the win goes to the players—40% goes to the counters, who do the lion's share of the work, and 10% is allocated according to the number of hours played by each BP. The counters' 40% is distributed in accordance with the number of hours played (20%), and on the amount won (20%).

I had scheduled plays for the four counter-BP pairs. Each BP had $7,000. Tony took Rambo to the Sands; Allen was playing with Frank at the Marina; Glynn was counting for Neil at the Imperial Palace. I took Robert to the Sundance.

It was conceivable that the bank could be doubled after these sessions, if each team won around $5,000. I was more than ready to take some time off, get out of Vegas, and relax for a few weeks in the Bay Area.

Robert and I found a double-deck game at the Sundance that was dealt way, way down. We played for over an hour before the count went high enough for me to signal a bet of more than $100.

Finally, the count soared. I gave the "chunk" signal. Robert put out two hands of $500. Two 13's against a ten. Robert hit both hands and busted.

Two more hands of $500. A 13 and 14 against a 10. We lost again.

As we kept playing, Robert was dealt stiff after stiff.*

The dealer was stuffing hundred dollar bills down the table chute as fast as Robert could pull them out of his pocket.

Robert was down to his last $500. In a gross breach of team security, I put $1,000 on the seat between Robert and me and kicked Robert under the table. He reached down and picked up the cash.

We hung on at that level for about an hour. Then the count went sky high once again. I signalled a $500 bet. Robert got a pair of 9's; the dealer had a 5 showing. I raised my thumb, and Robert split the 9's. On the first 9, Robert drew a ten. On the second 9, he drew another 9. Thumbs up, and Robert split again. Robert had $1,500 on the table and a solitary green chip in front of him. Robert pulled a ten and an ace. Things were looking good—he had two 19's and a 20.

The dealer had a ten in the hole. Still looking good. There were, I knew, plenty of tens in the deck, since the count was so high. The dealer drew a six, for 21.

We were tapped out.

I was still thinking positively in the cab on the way back to the Jockey Club. Perhaps the other guys did OK. And besides, Robert was now loved by the Sundance bosses, and he'd be able to get plenty of play there.

When I opened the condo door, I knew we were in trouble.

A glum Tony said, "Ken, please tell me you won!"

He and Rambo were sitting around the blackjack table; on the table was a meager handful of hundred dollar bills, all that was left of their $7,000.

I said, "We dropped eight."

Tony said, "Glynn lost, too."

Glynn's BP, Neil, had also tapped out. Worse yet, Glynn thought the Imperial Palace bosses had put him and Neil together. This meant

*A "stiff" is a poor hand, totaling between 12 and 16; a "pat" is a better hand, totaling 17 through 21.

possible heat, by proxy, on Tony and me, since we'd both played many sessions in the IP with Neil.

Between the three groups, we were down over $20,000. The only unknown was Allen and Frank, who were still out playing at the Marina.

We didn't know it at the time, but at that moment they were stuck nearly $5,000. They hung in there, and pulled out, ending up $1,100 winners.

The following day, Allen asked to talk to me privately.

"Ken, I think something's wrong. Last night, Frank and I changed tables, to move from the double-deck game to the single-deck game. I could swear he had over $2,000 on the table. When he got to the new table, he only had $1,500.

"And he took four breaks."

A few days earlier, I'd been with Frank at the Union Plaza. I thought he'd won $200 more than he reported. I shrugged off the discrepancy, assuming I'd missed a $200 cash-in somewhere along the line.

The counters are supposed to audit the BP's win or loss. But it's real tough for the counter to keep track of how much the BP cashes in for. The counter is under enormous pressure—he's making calculations, adjusting for aces, estimating the size of the discard pile, giving signals, making sure the dealer is dealing deep enough, and watching for heat from the pit.

In the heat of battle, say in the middle of a $1,000 double down, the counter's obviously concentrating on making sure he's calling the play accurately. He can easily miss the BP going in for more cash. In truth, more than not, I relied on the figure given to me by the BP. I'd sort of fake it when the BP told me how much he cashed in for, saying, "Yeah, that's what I counted, too."

I, too, had noticed that Frank tended to take a lot of breaks. And he sniffled a lot at the table. I assumed he'd done a little "toot" in the john, and several times told him, "No coke when you're playing. OK?"

"Ken, come on. I wouldn't do that."

Robert went back to the Sundance, this time with Tony. He checked into a huge suite on the top floor. A story was circulating in the casino that an Oriental woman had lost $200,000 there, and then won it all back, plus another $100,000. Maybe this little downtown club (which Tony inelegantly referred to as "The Toilet") would stand for some big action. We would see.

Glynn was counting for Frank at the Marina, and Allen and Jeff headed for Caesars.

## A Civilized Barring

Walking home after a play at Maxim's, I strolled through the air-conditioned MGM casino to get out of the 115-degree heat. The MGM is not a playable club; it has a terrible five-deck game, with two decks cut off.*

I noticed one dealer inserting the cutcard only one deck from the rear of the shoe. This was a beatable game. I stood behind the players, watching, for three shoes.

On the fourth shoe, the count went up; the deck favored the player by about 2%.

I sat down and bet $300, cash. A short, feral pit boss—he looked just like a fox—ran over and whispered something to the floorman watching the game. The floorman whispered to the dealer.

The dealer immediately pulled the cards out of the shoe. She shuffled them. Out of sheer obstinancy, I left out the $300 bet.

There were two other players at the table. The dealer dealt the round.

I drew an Ace, 7, versus the dealer's 5, and doubled down. I won the $600.

The floorman whispered to the dealer again.

The dealer picked up our cards, about twelve in all. She slid them into the discard pile, and pulled the undealt cards, about 4¾ decks, out of the shoe.

She shuffled.

Both players looked at the dealer, as if she were crazy.

One said, "What the hell's going on?"

*The MGM cutcard is generally inserted two decks from the rear of the shoe. The dealer pulls the cards out of the shoe and shuffles when he reaches the cutcard. Thus after only three decks are played, the cards are shuffled, which is totally unacceptable penetration.

The dealer shrugged, and said, "Just following orders."

Both players picked up their chips and left the table.

Obstinate to the end, I kept out a $300 bet. (This is stubborness, not intelligence. The shoe was about ½% against the player, at that point.)

I drew twenty against an ace. The dealer had blackjack.

She picked up my three black chips, my two cards, and her two cards—that's four cards out of 260 in the shoe (one card had also been "burned"). She pulled the remaining 255 cards out of the shoe.

It took her about a minute to shuffle the five decks.

I cut.

The dealer dealt one hand and repeated the entire process.

Some perverse rebelliousness caused me to stay at this table and watch the absurdity of it all, as the dealer dealt one round and shuffled, shuffled, and shuffled.

The pit ignored me. I ordered a drink, and kept "playing," cutting my bets back to $25.

Actually the house was "barring" me in a quite civilized manner. But my immaturity showed through, as I insisted on tying up a table and a dealer.

I asked the dealer, "Isn't this fun?"

She laughed. "Shuffling's good finger exercise."

She shrugged and rolled her eyes, as if to say, "What can I do?"

After 25 minutes, I tipped her a green chip and left the table.

This little charade does show that the casinos really don't have to bar counters. It demonstrated that there are more genteel ways of dealing with good players than saying, "Hit the door, pal."

While I was having fun, the team was getting blasted. Robert ran through yet another five grand at the Sundance. Tony called back to the condo, and Inga brought Robert another $5,000. He lost that, too.

Glynn had another complaint about Frank.

"He was in his suite, with some girl who couldn't have been 18. I called him on the house phone to come down to play. The girl came down with Frank, and cracked hundred-dollar bills at another table. Where'd she get that kind of money?"

Allen and Rambo came back from Caesars. They'd been up $5,000, and lost it all back, plus another $4,000.

I was wondering what the hell was going on. We went from up $30,000 to down over $15,000 in three days.

When counters or blackjack teams have extended losses, the talk inevitably seems to turn to external reasons. Our team was no exception, as we discussed whether we were being cheated, possible dishonesty on the team, and whether the casinos were shuffling the cards adequately enough to ensure that they were coming out randomly.

Actually, normal fluctuations in blackjack are enormous. Any counter who plays for an extended period of time will undergo huge downward swings. It's inevitable.

The main reason for this is because our edge is so tiny. Our group had about a 1% edge over the house. To put that figure in perspective, imagine a jar filled with 200 beans, 101 white beans and 99 black beans. If you pull out a white bean, you win your bet. If you pull out a black bean, you lose. After each "pull," the bean is replaced, and the next bet is made.

In the very long run, the excess of white beans over black beans will be felt. In the short (and not-so-short) run, however, it's entirely possible to pull out more black beans than white beans. It is this short-run that does in many counters and blackjack teams.

To put it in more practical terms, one of our counter-BP pairs could play full-time for an entire month, and still have a one out of five chance of being in the hole.* Similarly, if four counter-BP pairs played full-time for a week, they'd still have a 20% chance of losing.

The answer, of course, is to be adequately bankrolled, and to keep playing well, until the long run is finally reached. I don't know of a single player who, at one time or another, hasn't gotten discouraged and considered quitting. Once, two teammates, both excellent players, took $40,000 of my money and went to play in Belgium. After 61 days, playing full-time, they were down $30,000. That's discouraging. (They eventually came home winners.)

## The Best Blackjack Games in the World

Thanks to a pit boss at the Westward Ho casino, I ran into the very

*This assumes 35 hours per week, four weeks, and 70 hands per hour.

best blackjack game I'd ever played in my life—anywhere in the world.

Although I'd been read the Trespass Act at the "Ho" on a graveyard shift, I took a chance a few days later and returned to play their tempting single-deck game during swing. I planned to play the money myself, without a BP.

I started betting $5 per hand. No recognition in the pit. Graduated to green chips. Everything was still OK.

I lost hand after hand. This gave me a good excuse to "steam" up to three hands of $200 (their max bet). Before long, I was stuck $2,000.

I went in for another $2,000.

The boss, Paul, was truly friendly—not the superficial pit boss sycophancy which curries favor with high-rollers and lures "losing" action into the casino. Paul was sincerely sorry to see me losing so rapidly.

He whispered to me, "You know, there's always tomorrow."

In for another $2,000. I was down $6,000. Paul said, "We're having a special promotion, called Ho-waiian Luau. There's going to be a luau tomorrow. We're roasting a whole pig. Want to come?"

I said, "Sure".

Paul asked my name ("Billy Williams"), and if I'd have a guest ("Yes. Inga").

Two minutes later, Paul handed me a bag full of couponbooks, hats, and other assorted goodies.

I opened the coupon book and flipped through it. I almost fell off my chair. I was about to play the best blackjack game in the world!

By itself, the standard single-deck game at the Westward Ho is among the best in town. The Ho allows "Standard Strip Rules," which in effect means that the player is dead even off the top of the deck.*

Inside the coupon book were four coupons which allowed the player additional options at blackjack:

1. The player is paid 2 to 1 on blackjack.
2. The player does not lose on a total of 22.
3. The player wins 2 to 1 if he has a 5, 6, and 7 of the same suit.
4. The player wins automatically if he has 6 cards totaling 21 or less—even against a dealer blackjack.

*Standard Strip rules allow the player to double down on any two cards, and the dealer must hit soft 17.

The player gave the coupon to the dealer when he made each play. A player could get only one coupon book per day. Thus each option could be exercised once each day.

Then Paul came over. He said, "Billy. Let me give you a tip. But don't tell anyone I told you. When you double on 11 and get an ace, that counts as 22, too."

Paul was one sweet guy. What he meant was that the coupon could save the player twice as much if it was used on a "soft" 22 double down. Betting $200 per hand, that coupon alone would save us $400.

Rarely are there games that allow the non-counting player to have an edge over the house (assuming the player plays a well-known playing strategy, called Basic Strategy, which is described in the Appendix).

—As I write this, there's a game in Korea that gives the non-counting player a +.7% edge.

—Atlantic City once had an option called "early surrender," which allowed the player an edge of +.2%.

—Several years ago, Caesars Palace had a single-deck game that gave the player +.2% (with surrender and double down on split pairs).

But even those fabulous games couldn't compare with the Howaiian Luau single-deck game, played with the coupons.

Taken together, the Ho coupons gave the non-counting basic strategy player an incredible edge of beyond 3% over the house. The card-counter's advantage over the house was even higher.

I took a break—my head was buzzing from counting for four hours—and joined blackjack expert Arnold Snyder for dinner. Arnold had been in town and I had promised to show him our team operation. The team, fearing that something would show up in print, didn't want any media in our condos. I thoroughly trusted Arnold, but went along with the team vote.

At dinner we discussed the Ho's game. Arnold pointed out that the 2-for-1 blackjack coupon alone was worth 2.4% to the non-counting player. I drank a lot of booze and wine at dinner. I chug-a-lugged two cups of coffee, and we went to the Ho.

I started playing $200 a hand. In a few minutes, I got a blackjack. The dealer paid $400. How sweet that was.

I won another $1,000 or so back when someone sat down next to me and tapped me on the arm. It was Chuck Wenner, the Ho's Director of Casino Operations. Somehow, he'd found out I was there.

The jig was up. I had played against Chuck at the MGM, Stardust, the Treasury, and countless other places. Over the years, we'd become buddies.

"Kenny, what have you got against me?"

"Come on, Chuck. Let's sit down and have a drink."

He was mad. "No! Why the hell do you keep coming in here?"

"Come on, Chuck. Look at the bright side; you beat me for two grand."

"Dammit, Kenny, don't give me that."

"Look, Chuck. You offer these great games to everyone. Do you expect me to just ignore them?"

Chuck didn't see it my way. He turned red in the face. A friendship was about to be lost.

"If you come in here again, I swear, I'll have you arrested."

Now I got mad. I said, "No problem. I can train 'em faster than you can bar 'em," and stormed away.

When I got back to the Jockey Club, I called a counter training session.

"OK. It's time to pound the Ho. The special game's going to last five more days. Get the coupon books. Play $200 off the top. If the deck goes to minus 3 or worse, cut your bets back. At any plus count, go to three hands of $200.

"Don't use the blackjack coupon unless you have a $200 blackjack. And save the 22 coupon for $200 double downs."

In the next few days, Tony and Allen were barred at the Ho.

Rollie and I went to the Sands. I planned to play as a BP, since I'd been a high-roller there with Bob and his computer.

Rollie went into the casino to find a good double-deck game. I went to the front desk, gave the clerk $200 cash, and got a room under the name of Tommy Thompson.

I walked into the casino, sat at Rollie's table, and conspicuously placed my room key on the table (many bosses tend to relax when they know the player is a "legitimate" guest in the hotel). I threw $1,000 on the table and said to the boss, "OK, this trip I'm either going to win or lose ten grand."

The boss seemed to like the idea.

It was looking like it would be the latter. I put on the drunk act, and got a variation of $25 to $700. After a while, I asked the boss for a comp for four to their gourmet restaurant, The Regency Room. He was happy to oblige.

The play continued. Two big security guards were watching me. But they were on my side, guarding me against being hustled or ripped off by other customers. I turned and gave each of them two nickel chips, saying, "Thanks. This is for taking care of me." I joked, "Don't let me get hassled, especially by these bosses."

They thought that was hilarious.

(The intent, of course, was to get them on my side, in case serious heat came down. In the event of a barring, perhaps they'd be a little less militant.)

After a few hours, and $7,000 in cash, a boss tapped me on the shoulder.

"How much are you stuck, Kenny?"

It was Dick Butcher, a former Tropicana floorman, who had barred me there years ago.

I tried to bluff it, but knew it was all over.

"You got the wrong guy. My name's Thompson."

"Sure, Kenny."

I took my few chips and hustled out of the casino.

I didn't know it at the time, but Butcher's barring of me would threaten the very existence of our team.

# 13

# David Versus Several Goliaths

## The First Jolt

It was nine A.M. I'd just come back from a graveyard session at Caesars—five straight hours, half of it head-on. Talk about tired. I'd been buried $6,000 and dug out, was happy to walk away even.

A large manila envelope was in my Jockey Club mail box. The return address listed the Nevada Attorney General.

What did they want with me? Did it have something to do with the card-counting lawsuit?

Inside was some kind of a legal document, full of all kinds big words. I suddenly understood what it was and almost hit the floor.

"COMES NOW the NEVADA GAMING COMMISSION, by and through its counsel BRIAN McKAY, Attorney General, moves this Court to dismiss the petition for judicial review."

Incredible! The Attorney General's representing the Commission! They had filed a Motion To Dismiss my petition for a Court hearing.

What the hell's going on?

I thought Attorney Generals (I know, it's supposed to be Attorneys

General, but I don't talk that way) were independent agencies that made sure everyone enforced the law. The Attorney General in New Jersey, after reviewing my case, had even testified for us before their Supreme Court.

Thinking the Nevada AG was an objective law enforcement agency, I had written them earlier, telling them that the Commission broke the law by not responding to my petition within the legal time limit. I had hoped that the Attorney General would put pressure on the Commission.

Naïve.

It's frightening and intimidating when you see a Motion directed right at YOU, on Attorney General stationery, signed by the Attorney General and his Deputy Attorney Generals. It doesn't make you feel like you're fighting City Hall—more like holding off the State Government, or the National Guard.

I didn't even want to guess how many lawyers there were in the Attorney General's Office.

I started reading the motion and felt even worse. The lengthy document was full of gibberish, such as:

"See Sprague Oil Service, Inc. v. Fadely, 189 Kan. 23, 367 P.2d 56 (1961); see also Colorado-Ute Electric Association, Inc. v. Air Pollution Control Commission, 41 Colo. App. 293, 591 P.2d 1323 (1979), rev'd on other grounds sub nom. CF & I Steel Corp. v. Colorado Air Pollution Control Commission, 199 Colo. 273, 610 P.2d (1980), on remand, 640 P.2d 238 (Colo. App. 1981), cert. dismissed sub nom."

And this was the text, not footnotes.

I was beginning to feel I was definitely out of my league.

I went up to the condo, threw the Motion on a two-foot pile of legal papers, and went to sleep so I'd be ready to play swing shift.

I'd worry about it when the time came.

## Jolt Number Two

Three days later, there was another envelope in the mailbox. This time it wasn't from the Attorney General, it was from the Nevada Resort Association. You remember? That's the outfit that represents

Caesars, Golden Nugget, the Hilton, the MGM, and just about every other casino in town—i.e., another City Hall.

I had a feeling what was inside.

I pulled out a document, a Motion To Intervene. They wanted in in the battle, too.

Then, I found another Motion To Dismiss my petition. It was even thicker than the Attorney General's and full of just as much gibberish.

There was yet another document, entitled, "Proposed Memorandum of the Nevada Resort Association In Support of Respondent's Motion To Dismiss Petition."

In other words, the NRA's supporting the Attorney General, who's representing the Commission, who ruled against me, 5 to 0.

At this point, I wasn't feeling very loved in Nevada.

I leafed through this last document and saw things like "Estes v. Nevada, James v. Churchill Downs, Inc., Winfield v. Noe, State v. Rosenthal, O'Callaghan v. Eighth Judicial District Court, Bush v. City of Wichita"—and over 20 more references.

It'd take me the rest of the year to look up all these citations, let alone even begin to understand them and compose a rebuttal.

I had the uncomfortable feeling that the Nevada lawsuit was coming to a rapid end.

Not only was the subject complicated, but I was fighting the whole damn state—the casinos, the government agencies, the law enforcement agencies, and the casino associations. To say nothing of our team's daily battle with shuffling dealers, floormen, pit bosses, and Griffin agents.

It didn't help that our team had gone down another eleven grand in the last 24 hours.

## A Phone Call Motivates

A phone call came in that infuriated me, pumped a little energy into me, and got me working once again with some enthusiasm on the legal project.

A counter named Allen Brown phoned. He and a friend, Barry Finn, were playing black ($100) chips at the Horseshoe.

In addition to counting, Allen and Barry were doing something called "first-basing." This technique involves playing at "first base" (the far right seat) at a blackjack table, and peeking at the hole card as the dealer checks it to see if he has a blackjack.

The player then varies how he plays his hand, depending on whether the dealer has a "pat" hand (totalling 17 through 20), or a "stiff" hand (12 through 16).

First-basers have a healthy edge over the house, up to 2%. If card-counting techniques are also used, the edge is even higher, 3% or more.*

Allen and Barry were eventually spotted and rushed into a back office by several security guards. (Next time you're at the Horseshoe, check out the guards. They're the burliest, meanest-looking goons you've ever laid eyes on.)

Here's how Allen told it to me:

"I've been playing since 1972. I was first-basing with Barry. They restricted us to a flat bet, but we were still beating them. As I was leaving, a security guard grabbed me. He said, 'I want to talk to you.'

" 'Fine.'

"He started to drag me toward a back room.

"I said, 'Let's talk here.'

" 'You don't have a choice.'

"He put a headlock on me and dragged me into the backroom.

"A few minutes later, they dragged Barry in, too.

"There were five or six guards in the room, three in uniform. All of them were 225 pounds or more. One of them said:

" 'Let's beat the hell out of them.'

"They knocked us down. Several were wearing cowboy boots and they started kicking and stomping us. One guy grabbed a walking cane and hit me in the head with it.

"Another pulled a gun out of his holster—although he didn't point it at us.

"During the beating, I crapped my pants.

"After 20 or 25 minutes, they took us out to the street and let us go.

*I've never written about first-basing until now, because players who have been using this technique have asked me not to. These players have been retired for several years and I'm now free to write about first-basing, and have described first-basing experiences in subsequent chapters.

"There was a third counter with us who got away. One guard said, 'We're looking for the other guy. When we find him, we're gonna give him the same treatment.'

"I could still walk, and we drove to my condo. When I got home, I couldn't move. The guys called the paramedics and I went to the hospital. My blood pressure had really dropped.

"I had five broken ribs, a ruptured spleen, and contusions on my liver, kidney and lung. There were black-and-blue bruises all over my body.

"I've been in the hospital since Friday night (five days). Tomorrow they're giving me a SCAT scan to check on my ruptured spleen." (It turned out Allen's spleen was severely bruised, but not ruptured.)

Barry got off easy—he had only three broken ribs.

Later I was told that Allen almost didn't make it.

Yes, they're suing—for 3 million (their lawyer, Les Combs, by coincidence, was a former blackjack teammate of mine).

It seems incredible that in 1985, this kind of primitive behavior can still happen.

Despite this horror story, we're still the huge underdogs in our legal battle. It doesn't make sense.

## The Opposition to the Motions To Dismiss

The Court hearing was a week away. It was time to prepare some kind of opposition to all those Motions To Dismiss, or just lie down and give up.

I didn't begin to try to understand the Motions To Dismiss, let alone go to a law library and spend days looking up their references.

Instead I concentrated on the statutes. I had hoped, regardless of all the citations, that the law basically said that a guy could go to court if he felt the Commission gave him a raw deal.

So I just wrote a common argument, which went like this:

1. I was aggrieved by the Commission.
2. The law says a "person aggrieved" can ask for his day in court.
3. I'm asking for my day in court.
4. If you don't give it to me, you're making the Commission all-powerful. Even this court is subject to appeal; isn't the Commission?

My "Opposition To Motion To Dismiss" was only five pages,

double-spaced. I didn't cite a single court case. I didn't know any to cite.

That night while lying in bed trying to sleep, I figured I'd blown the case. God knows what those dozens of precedents cited by the opposition meant.

I had heard a rumor that this judge, when he was a lawyer, had represented the Griffin agency.

Then I thought, "What's the difference? Even if I did the research, no matter how well I argued, I'm fighting a Nevada judge, too."

It reminded me of another scene from the Sakharov movie. The Sakharov's were sitting in court, trying to introduce some relevant text into the record. The Soviet judge cut them off, saying: "The Court will read your evidence in the way it considers necessary."

Well, let the chips fall where they may. It's time to go play some blackjack.

The next day, I put on my business suit (the only one I owned—I can't stand them) and went down to the Courthouse. It took five minutes to file the opposition papers.

On impulse, I walked down to Vegas's main drag, Fremont Street, and strolled into the Horseshoe Casino. I spotted an empty table, put my leather attaché case on a chair, and threw $500 on the table.

The dealer announced, "Changing $500."

The boss came over, took one quick, uninterested glance at me, and walked away.

Now if I were dressed the casual way I usually am when playing, the boss would be watching to make sure I was "all right."

Obviously the suit and the attaché case helped. The fact that it was around noon, I believe, made it appear that I was just some Vegas businessman on lunch hour, stopping in to a play a few hands.

I dropped the $500. Cashed in another $500, duly recorded by the boss, who yelled, "OK," not even looking at the table.

I played 30 minutes, won $700, cashed in, and walked out the door, without a reaction from anyone in the casino.

The Vegas-lawyer-with-a-gambling-habit-on-his-lunch-hour had made his debut.

# 14

# Regrouping—Back to the Drawing Boards

Two days after Butcher spotted me at the Sands, Rollie and Tony took Robert to Maxim's. They planned to play at adjacent tables. Robert would hop back and forth, as the decks got hot.

After playing for an hour, the Shift Manager, Nick Gullo, came over to Robert, who had asked for a comp. Instead of a comp, Robert got barred.

Nick showed Robert pictures of him playing with Rollie and Tony, taken from the sky.

Nick said, "We know that these guys are always with you when you play."

Then he said, "Tell Kenny hello for me," giving Robert his business card.

Robert said, "Kenny, who?"

Rollie left the casino before he could get barred. Tony was just walking out the door when Gullo come up to him and said, "We don't want your action in here any more."

Tony responded, "Listen, Pal. I don't want your action either."

We couldn't figure out why Gullo had suspected that the group had anything to do with me.

The mystery was solved a few hours later, when I got a call from a friend of Rollie's, who had lived in Vegas for years. He knew casino bosses all over town, including several at the Sands. He said, "Butcher was the only one who recognized you. I'm not surprised; he was a cop for ten years, before he went to work in the casinos.

"Butcher's a friend of Bob Griffin. He gave your picture, and Rollie's, to the Griffin Agency. Griffin sent fliers all over town with the pictures."

Rollie's friend went on, "The guy who wrote your comp to the Regency Room is the laughing-stock of the Strip. He's lucky he didn't lose his job."

He continued, "I was in the Trop today. A pit boss showed me a stack of pictures of your team. He said, 'Kenny, the Hatchetman, is back in town.' I pretended I didn't know who he was talking about."

Talk about guilt by association. Rollie got heat because he was counting for me at the Sands. Then Rollie "dirtied" Robert by playing with him at Maxim's. Tony, in turn, got barred because he was photographed playing with Robert.

The entire chain of events was started because Butcher gave pictures to the Griffin agency. I thought, "Why couldn't he have been content just to bar me at the Sands?"

Over the next few days, Robert was barred at the IP, the Trop, the Sands, and Caesars. Tony was hustled into the back room at the Flamingo Hilton and forced to have his picture taken. He went downtown to play; the instant he sat down at the Union Plaza he was barred. Fifteen minutes later, he was thrown out of the Mint.

Rollie's picture was taken with Robert at Bourbon Street. Through an inside contact at Caesars, Rollie found out that this picture, too, had also been circulated to the casinos by the Griffin agency.

I continued to schedule plays for them at the safer clubs. Strangely, I personally wasn't getting much heat at all. Neither was Glynn, Allen, Neil or Inga.

But the team wasn't making progress. After a week, we pulled back to even. Then, in another disastrous day, we lost $23,000.

It seemed as if we'd never get this bank doubled. Tony kept running into more trouble. He and Robert were barred on sight at the Riviera (which had recently become playable, switching from five decks to two). In a single day, Tony was detained in two back rooms, at the Imperial Palace and the Sands. He was finding it hard to get a game anywhere in town.

Eventually Tony flew back to Philly. He hoped to get some play back in Atlantic City. We knew, however, that the Griffin book was also circulated to at least one AC club, Caesars.

I did an analysis of Frank's play, versus the other BP's. None of the BP's results were particularly impressive. However, Frank had lost, by far, the largest amount of all the BP's. It was difficult to tell if this was "statistically significant," given the small number of hands the team had played. But, given other suspicions, I considered gently disassociating ourselves from him.

Frank and I put on a play at the Marina a few days later which made up my mind. At this point, I had come to strongly suspect that, not only did Frank use coke, but that the source of the hundred dollar bills that he threw around when I first met him came from dealing the stuff. Frank had a beeper which often went off at odd times of the day and night.

About a half-hour into the play, I noticed Frank's hands shaking. He'd been nervous on previous plays, especially when he first started with us. But now he was more nervous than ever and he seemed totally uneasy—almost as if he was afraid of the people in the pit. He continually stared into the pit. His face had the guilty look of a criminal caught in the act; he looked so suspicious that I called off the play.

I stayed at the table for ten minutes after Frank quit, and went up to his suite. He had a pile of coke on the cocktail table and a rolled up hundred dollar bill. His pupils were dilated. He was obviously stoned.

I said, "Frank. We've got to talk. This stuff's affecting your play."

He said, "Ken, look, I had some trouble with my wife this afternoon, so I got high. I was coming down off the stuff at the table and just got paranoid."

Frank gave me the bankroll—around $7,000. I peeled off $1,000 and gave it to him, saying "This is for services rendered. We'll cool it for a while. I'll give you a call sometime."

That was our last play with Frank.

Rollie also stopped playing in Vegas; he was getting more heat with our team than he'd ever gotten individually. He decided to go abroad for a while, and play on his own, hoping that he'd "cool off" in Vegas after a few months.

It was time to regroup. I went back to San Francisco to reflect on what was happening.

The 1985 blackjack game was a lot different than it was when we'd played earlier. In the old days, we'd double banks, on average, in nine days. Now, things were different:

—Pit bosses were much more knowledgable about card-counting, were better able to spot counters, and were far more suspicious of large bet variation.

—More casinos took counter-measures, such as inserting the cutcard further from the end of the shoe (*e.g.*, the Desert Inn and MGM), shuffling hand-held games earlier (*e.g.*, the Circus and Stardust), or shuffling when a big bet was put out (random dealers in all casinos).

We found that Oriental dealers often shuffled more. This view was universally held by our teammates and by many other counters as well. Once, I asked a shift manager about this. He said, "We don't tell them to do this. But Oriental dealers do protect the games better. They're ambitious; they're company people; they want to do a good job. They know counters place big bets out when the player has the edge. So they shuffle up."

Our players found this was the case at casinos all over town. So we generally stayed away from Oriental dealers, unless they'd been observed dealing good games.

—Our edge was much smaller than in the past. Not only did we win at a lower rate, but the expected fluctuations were more extreme.

Because of our much lower edge, I formulated a new, larger bank. Between Glynn, Allen, Neil, myself and several outside investors, we put together a bank of $125,000. This time we'd be ultra-conservative, playing to what we call a 3% element-of-ruin.*

Further, we couldn't expect to double the bank in a few weeks. We would play for the long term, recognizing that we were involved in a project lasting several months or longer.

*The higher the bet size, the greater the chance of going broke. I adjusted the size of our betting, given our $125,000, so that, statistically, we had a 3% chance of going broke (i.e., element-of-ruin), and a 97% chance of doubling the $125,000.

We would conduct our operation in secrecy. We moved out of the Jockey Club, where just about every resident knew my team was in action. Our team often ate together, and we spent a lot of time, after sessions, drinking and playing video games in the Jockey Club lounge.

We would tell no one when or where we were playing. We rented a Vegas apartment and kept its location a team secret.

We would not play as intensively in Vegas as we had earlier. We'd play for five or six days at a time. Then we'd take time off. Periodically we'd go to Reno or Lake Tahoe. The players with the most heat, Tony, Robert, and Rollie, would no longer be with us. We hoped that the casino and Griffin people would think the team was out of business.

Glynn and I got disguises.

Allen was still able to play virtually anywhere. For BP's, we'd use Rambo, Neil, and Inga. Two San Francisco businessmen wanted to be BP's. One, the owner and president of a medium-sized company, looked and acted like a gambler; he talked with a gruff, eastern accent and liked to wear gaudy gold jewelry. He'd be particularly convincing in the casinos. Another counter, Doug, was still in training in San Francisco.

## New Techniques

I worked out some new concepts that would make our play far stronger.

### *Discard Pile Improvements*

Years ago, the best games in Vegas were the single- and four-deck games. Single deck was preferable, because mathematically it was the most profitable; we played four deck because we could apply the team approach (many counters and one BP) that had started me in blackjack. We rarely played double deck.

Now things were different. Double-deck games constituted by far the best opportunity in Vegas. Nearly all single-deck games were closely watched and offered little earnings opportunity. But there were highly beatable two-deck games all over town—at the Hacienda,

Trop, Sands, Marina, Imperial Palace, Riviera, Maxim's, Sahara, Sundance, and Union Plaza.

I worked out new training techniques that would allow us to play the double-deck game more accurately. First, I put together six packs of cards; they contained 13, 26, 39, 52, 65, and 78 cards (corresponding to ¼, ½, ¾, 1, 1¼, and 1½ decks, respectively).

These packs represented what the counter would see in the discard pile. On top of each pack I wrote the number of aces that should have been played, assuming a pack of that size was seen in the discard pile. For example, on the 26-card (½ deck) pack, I wrote 2 aces, because if 26 cards are dealt, the "normal" number of aces played is two (since there is one ace per 13 cards).

I also wrote, on each pack, the factor to convert the running count to the true count.*

I put the packs on a table and mixed them up randomly. Going from left to right, I would then recite the number of "normal" aces and the conversion factor that applied to each pack.

Allen, Glynn and I trained, using this technique. As we practiced, it became obvious that all three of us had tended in the past to underestimate the size of the discard pile. That meant that we were making inaccurate betting calculations; both our ace adjustment and true count conversions were off.

At first this went quite slowly. After about three hours, however, we found that our eyes had become "calibrated," and we could determine the number of aces and the conversion factor rapidly and accurately.

*We converted our "running count" to a "true count" to reflect how many cards remain to be played. We did this by dividing the running count by the number of half-decks remaining to be played (the "conversion factor"). For example, in a double-deck game, if there were 26 cards in the discard pile, there were 1½ decks (or 3 half-decks) to be played. Thus the conversion factor was 3. The packs I put together were as follows:

| *Cards* | *Half Decks To be Played* | *"Normal" Aces* | *Conversion Factor* |
|---|---|---|---|
| 13 | 3½ | 1 | x .3 |
| 26 | 3 | 2 | / 3 |
| 39 | 2½ | 3 | x .4 |
| 52 | 2 | 4 | / 2 |
| 65 | 1½ | 5 | x .8 |
| 78 | 1 | 6 | / 1 |

In the past, playing four-deck games, our teams had made these calculations only to the nearest ½ deck, or 2 aces.

*Changes in Betting Formula*

I had been supplied some recent blackjack studies conducted by computer expert Stanford Wong. Wong's studies showed that penetration was for more important than we'd thought previously. We were aware, as were all blackjack pros, that with the same true count the player has a greater edge the further down in the deck or pack he is.

However, the newer studies showed that we'd underestimated the importance of this factor. Further, the studies gave much more specific data than had ever been previously available.

Depending on the size of our bank at the time, we had always bet according to such formulas as "the true count in black chips," or "the true count times 3 greens." These formulas totally disregarded Wong's penetration conclusions.

We looked into ways to build this penetration effect into our betting. At first, we thought we'd take advantage of the fact that, with a given true count, the larger the discard pile, the larger the bet.

Then we came up with what I thought was an ingenious idea, one that we'd never even considered in the past, to allow us automatically to bet more when we were further into the pack.

We increased the number of "normal" aces, when 1¼ decks had been dealt (in a two-deck game). The number of normal aces for 1¼ decks became an intentionally spurious 6 (instead of 5). For 1½ decks, it was 7 (instead of 6). This adjustment increased the amount bet by the effect of one ace.

This scheme automatically built in a penetration adjustment, and required absolutely no additional work at the table by our counters.

We changed the numbers written on the ¼-deck packs accordingly and practiced some more.

*Number of Players at the Table*

Wong's studies had also shown that the fewer players at the table, the greater the earnings rate per hand.

We, of course, had known that the player gets more hands per hour at an empty table than at a full one. Obviously, playing 200 hands per hour in a head-on game won almost three times as much as playing 70 hands per hour at a full table.

But recent studies revealed that the winning *rate* also increases with fewer players. Wong had simulated millions of hands on a computer. The simulations showed that, for a given count, the earnings potential was higher with fewer players at the table. Once again, the study results were published in great detail, showing detailed earnings rates, quantifying the magnitude of this factor.

The conclusions made sense. In a double-deck game, for example, the proportion of unprofitable freshly-shuffled hands (in which the player has about a .4% disadvantage) is much higher than if the player were playing, say, head-on.

Because of this, we changed our approach. We adopted two new methods, which we called "counter-counter" and "on-the-rail" play, to reduce the average number of players at our tables.

### *Counter-Counter Play*

We would send two counters out together (call them Counter A and Counter B). Counter A would be the BP, not look at the cards, and take signals from Counter B. They'd find an empty table, with good penetration.

When the boss felt comfortable with Counter A as a typical losing high-roller, Counter B would leave the table. Counter A would pick up the count and play head-on.

When the bosses started watching Counter A closely, Counter B would return to the table and pick up the count, allowing Counter A to look away from the cards and put on his act again.

### *On the Rail*

I developed signals for counters to signal BP's without having to play and thus take up a hand. This would allow the BP to play, on average, with fewer players, and even, play head-on.

Betting signals were based on locating the hand on the body. The higher the location, the higher the bet, as follows:

| | |
|---|---|
| Hand on tummy | 1 chip |
| Hand on chest | 2 chips |
| Hand on mouth | 3 chips |
| Hand on top of head | 4 chips |

We'd use the same signals for play of the hands that we were using (thumb and index together, hit; apart, stand; thumb up, double or split). The only difference would be that the counter's hand, instead of resting on the table, would be on his chest, against the back of a chair, or in any other convenient, but natural-looking, location. For insurance, the counter would turn his back on the table.

We called this signaling technique playing "on-the-rail," from the old poker term.

On-the-rail playing offered the additional advantage of allowing the BP to change tables more frequently. If other players, as well as our counter, followed a high-rolling BP to the new table, so much the better. Our counter would blend in with the crowd.

The counter, standing up, could also better assess what was going on in the pit. Rather than being part of the action, and perhaps drawing heat, the counter was merely a casual observer. He could freely look at the BP, the floorman watching the game, or any bosses watching the game from a distance. To stay cool, the counter would turn his back on the game in between shuffles and whenever cards were not being turned over.

*Photo-madness in Vegas*

I'd found that Vegas in 1985 was different in another way—the casinos relied much more heavily on photos. Nearly every club in town had dozens of little domes which contained hidden cameras, mounted on the ceiling. Some clubs even had the cameras trained on non-playing areas, such as hallways, bars, and elevator entrances.

The surveillance had never been this intense before.

Some casinos relied more heavily on the cameras than others—and often tipped their hand. For example, at clubs like the Flamingo Hilton, the Landmark, and the Stardust, at the first sign of an unknown high-roller, a boss in the pit would often pick up the phone. If the boss didn't start hawking the game closely, it was fairly obvious that someone upstairs was watching.

Bosses in other clubs, such as the Imperial Palace and Riviera, did not phone. They watched closely from the pit. In the latter case, the counter could call "cover" (misleading) bets and plays. If and as the boss relaxed and walked away from the game, we could revert to our normal play.

When clubs relied on the "sky," we had to guess when we were being watched. We'd employ cover—keeping bet variation to a minimum—until the boss received a call (which, we assumed, was the sky calling down to say, "This guy's OK"). If no call came, the counter would keep the cover going for 15 or 20 minutes—and gradually move into our planned playing strategy.

I knew that most photography was in black and white. (We could often see photos of undesirable players Scotch-taped to the pit stands.) Thus, I instructed our BP's in ways to mix colors and get betting ratios more unobtrusively. A $100 bet could be 3 greens and 4 reds (which was close enough). A $400 bet would be 3 blacks, 3 greens, and a red. (Both betting stacks were 7 chips high.) We developed a series of different combinations of chip colors, which approximated our betting strategy. The BP's memorized these combinations.

This would make it more difficult for the sky people to determine exactly how much our BP's were betting—either while watching the play or when viewing the re-runs (another recent surveillance technique that we discovered the casinos were using). We'd hoped the sky would get so confused trying to total the bets that they'd be unable to relate it to the way the "deck was moving."

*Reducing Heat*

I'd found that the casinos cooperated with each other more than they had in the past. In fact, the Dunes' Vic Vickery, in a speech to industry people, had recently urged the formation of an inter-casino surveillance system to protect all casinos in town from credit scams and dishonest players. I didn't doubt for a minute that such a network would soon be expanded into an Electronic Griffin Book, featuring known card-counters.

Tony, Rollie, and Robert had brought each other heat because of the circulation of photos by Griffin or the exchange of photos from one casino to another. While I couldn't do anything to prevent photos being taken from the sky, I did believe that we could prevent the better quality, and thus more damaging, back-room polaroid photos from being taken.

My Vegas legal research made it clear that various card-counter lawsuits (some handled by ex-teammate Les Combs), had established that the detention of a person, against his will, in a back room constituted what the lawyers called "false arrest." Requiring someone to show identification, or taking pictures of him without his permission, constituted what was called "invasion of privacy." It was widely known that casinos had been sued, and had settled out of court, for precisely these kinds of violations.

We developed a new "heat strategy." All our counters and BP's, if stopped, would be courteous and polite, to a fault. If told to go to a back room, they would say, "My lawyer has advised me that this is 'false arrest.' If you force me, I will hold the casino, as well as you personally, legally liable."

We would use the phrase "invasion of privacy" if ID or photos were mentioned.

This legalese, I had hoped, might minimize the circulation of polaroids of the team around Vegas.

I Xeroxed and distributed copies of NRS 463.151, which listed the types of persons that could be excluded from casinos (known felons, tax evaders, and the like). I hoped that a teammate, displaying a copy of the Nevada statutes, would cause security guards and casino bosses to have second thoughts before hassling him.

Our new bank was formed. Our team had fresh new faces. We were ready for action, once again.

# 15

# A New Start

Our group taxied to the San Francisco airport in two cabs. There was Glynn, Allen, Rambo, and $40,000 in one cab; Neil, Inga, I, and $50,000 in the other. The remainder of the $125,000 bank stayed in San Francisco, in a safety deposit box.

We settled in our three-bedroom Vegas apartment. We set up a blackjack table, pulled out our flash cards and deck packs, and practiced for a few hours.

On our very first play, I took Neil to the Sundance and called plays for him on-the-rail. The play worked better than we had hoped.

Neil sat down at a table with one other player. He cashed in for $1,000 and sat sideways in his chair, so he could naturally glance to his right. I stood behind a chair at first base. I placed my right hand on the inside of the back of the chair and moved my thumb and finger subtly, to transmit the playing signals to Neil. The boss, standing near me and watching Neil, couldn't see my hand.

On-the-rail counting was much easier than sitting at the table. For one thing, I didn't have to make bets and play my own hands. More importantly, I felt far more comfortable, since there was absolutely no heat on me. From my standing vantage point, I felt I was observing the boss, rather than vice versa.

When the last round of each two-deck pack had been played, I turned to watch the game at the table behind me. I didn't turn back to Neil's table until after the dealer had shuffled, dealt the next round, and Neil picked up his cards. I also ignored Neil's game during changes of color, during "fills" of the chip rack, and whenever cards were not being turned over. I discovered that when counting on-the-rail, the counter had to actually watch the BP's game less than half the time.

Neil, who was playing a top bet of "two five's" (two hands of $500), went up $2,500 almost immediately. Spectators gathered around to watch. Neil was chatting amiably with the pit boss. He continued to win. He was up over $4,000, when the boss picked up the pit phone. Since I was standing, I could readily see around the entire casino. I noticed a large man in an adjacent pit, whom I knew to be the shift manager, pick up the phone. He immediately looked over at Neil's table.

The shift manager conferred with another boss, and both men walked out of their pit and approached Neil's table. They squeezed by me, not even looking at me, saying, "Excuse me," and entered Neil's pit. The dealer was shuffling. I decided to place a "cover bet," and touched the top of my head. Neil put out five black chips on the new shuffle.

Neil was now being watched by three bosses and over a dozen spectators standing in the aisle. I inched a bit to my left to blend in with the crowd (if I moved too far to the left, Neil would have had to glance at me more obviously).

Neil lost the hand, and the count went up. I signaled another top bet. Throughout this shuffle, the count, while not astronomically high, stayed sufficiently above zero to justify $500 bets. Even though Neil was now apparently flat-betting, the shift manager didn't seem to relax. The dealers didn't check the hole card at the Sundance, so I knew the boss wasn't concerned with spooking or first-basing.* Thus

*Until recently, Nevada dealers checked their holecard if they had a ten or ace upcard, to see if they had a blackjack. They did this because, when the dealer had a blackjack, it wasn't necessary for the players to play out their hands—all players, except those who also had a blackjack, automatically lost.

When the dealer checks his holecard, he knows whether he has a "pat" or "stiff" hand. This can lead to several abuses. First, a dishonest dealer can signal this information to a player or confederate, who can adjust his play accordingly. For example, they weren't convinced that Neil wasn't a counter, or perhaps they thought he was a card-marker or some other form of cheat.

I kept the play going. Neil's audience was getting even larger, and spectators were starting to jostle me. I had to continually elbow myself into a better position, to maintain line-of-sight with Neil. The count went down. Rather than drawing possible heat by giving Neil a $50 or $100 bet, I gave him the take-a-break signal.

When Neil stood up, the two bosses left the pit. Most of the crowd remained, expecting play to resume, since Neil's many stacks of black chips were still on the table.

Neil came back five minutes later, and we started playing again. Dammed if the two bosses didn't return too.

One play in particular cooled Neil off. He had a $500 bet out. The dealer shuffled. I gave Neil an improvised "super-chunk" bet by holding my hand way above my head (granted, not the most natural signal in the world, but no one was looking at me). Neil got the message. He put out another hand of $500.

He lost both hands. That did it. The two bosses walked away.

Neil went on to win $7,500 at the Sundance and was given a suite. The bosses had no idea what had hit them.

In this case, Neil's action of raising his bet when caught with a $500 bet out, did the job for him. All counters occasionally encounter a shuffle-up with a top bet out. Novice counters, faced with that situation, often withdraw their big bet and replace it with a smaller one. Most dealers and bosses, seeing this, immediately identify the player as a counter.

Withdrawing a big bet is considered such a blatant sign of card-counting that even our BP's, drunk and not watching the cards, had

if the dealer had a stiff hand, and the player had a 16, the player would not hit his 16, since the dealer has a high likelihood of busting. If the dealer had a pat hand of 17 or above, the player, obviously, would take a hit.

Second, players could surreptitiously peek at the holecard, and adjust their play accordingly. This can be done by stationing a confederate to the rear of the dealer, who signals "pat" or "stiff" across the pit to the player at the table ("spooking"). Another technique is to have a player at first base (usually standing, to get a better angle) peeking at the holecard ("first-basing").

To avoid these abuses, many Nevada casinos instructed their dealers not to check for blackjack when they had a ten valued upcard (4 out of 5 occurrences, or 80% of the time). Dealers continued to check if they had an ace upcard, so they could settle insurance bets which were placed by the players.

drawn heat by pulling back big bets. As a result, we had a team policy against this.

I'd noticed that some counters, when caught with a big bet out, would make some excuse and leave the table, either for another table or the rest room. This, too, often draws heat. It also tends to lower earnings, since just to pull back one big bet, play is interrupted (and the number of hands played is reduced).

A diversion that we once used was to pull back the bet, pretend to count chips during the break in the action, and then put out a smaller bet. This worked years ago, when the bosses' knowledge of counting was limited. In 1985, however, not many bosses and dealers would be fooled by this.

We established a team policy of handling this problem in one of three ways:

1. Leave the bet out, and act as if the shuffle didn't matter in the least.

2. Split the bet into 2 or 3 bets. Thus the boss sees the same amount of money out. Mathematically, however, three bets of, say, $100 constitutes a much smaller risk than one bet of $300.

3. *Increase* the size of the bet, as Neil did. We'd found that if the BP makes this minimal sacrifice once or twice, he's often securely established as a non-counter.

If the player has a .5% disadvantage off the top and makes two bets of $500, the actual sacrifice, on average, is only $5. It's certainly worth paying a few $5's to get hours and hours of additional play, worth $200 to $400 per hour.

A few weeks earlier at the Royal Las Vegas, I had come out, on occasion, with $200 after the shuffle.

Shortly after, I overheard one boss ask the other, his superior, "Do you think he's counting?"

The boss replied, "No way. He bets $200 off the top."

Whenever that boss came by the table, I'd try to make sure he saw an off-the-top bet of $200. Hours later, he comped me into the hotel, as Tommy Thompson. "Tommy" was to play the Royal for weeks, before finally getting shuffled up on.

At the Royal, the cover bets entailed absolutely no sacrifice, since their single-deck game was dead even off the top. Yet that one ploy not only resulted in dozens of hours of play at that club, but led the pit to relax about penetration.

When the dealers know the pit likes you, they relax and often deal further down in the deck. The Royal dealers were giving me 40 to 45 cards out of 52, which is incredible penetration for Vegas. One dealer dealt an incredible three rounds with five players at the table—something we rarely encountered even when we were playing years ago.

The following day, we tried our second new technique—the Counter A, Counter B approach. I put on the new disguise—a gray wig and eyeglasses—and went with Allen to the Hacienda. We found an empty double-deck game. I played $2 per hand for five minutes. Then I signaled for Allen to sit down.

Allen came over, cashed in a thousand and started betting green chips. He stood at the table, and looked around the casino, checking people out, eyeing cocktail waitresses, and, of course, ignoring the cards.

A female pit boss watched the game warily. She ordered a rack of black chips for Allen. Allen put out $300, and the dealer shuffled. Allen capped the bet with two quarters.

Allen, normally sedate, was putting on a good act. He'd slam the table when he lost a hand; cheer when he won. He was making a lot of noise. He was also losing.

Allen and I were the only players at the table.

Finally the pit boss introduced herself to Allen, asked his name, and uttered the standard, "Let me know if you need anything." She walked away, not bothering to watch the game any longer.

Allen was "in." I left the table, and Allen started counting for himself. It was delightful to be able to walk away from the table in the middle of a play and know everything was under control. With a BP, we obviously could not do this.

So Allen took over. I strolled around the casino, played a hand or two at several different tables, and chatted with some gal pulling a slot machine.

Now Allen had a nice head-on game, getting in about 200 hands per hour. He was also benefiting from the additional potential win rate that comes from head-on play. Despite this, he kept losing.

No one was watching Allen's play. I left him alone until 25 minutes later, when the female boss returned to hawk the game some more. I sat down and started counting and signaling, so Allen could, once again, be observed ignoring another player's cards. (When the counter is playing alone, the bosses cannot tell whether he's interested in other player's cards, because the only cards he sees are his own and the dealer's, and obviously all players look at their own cards and those of the dealer.)

Spectators started watching Allen. The count went sky high. Allen put out $500. I didn't want to use up cards during this highly favorable situation. I said to a spectator, loudly, "He makes me too nervous," pocketed my chips, and joined the spectators, watching the game.

We found we placed far more big bets out per hour with this technique, which we called "reverse card-eating."*

For the rest of the pack, I gave Allen signals on-the-rail. He was now betting $500 per hand, head-on. When he won, we were all cheering.

Finally when the decks ran out, I left and went to play at the next table. It was Allen's turn to start counting again.

I looked over and saw Allen had $25 bets out. Thus I knew the count was negative. I re-joined him, betting $2 per hand—eating up cards in this undesirable situation. After the shuffle, I took up the count once again.

A few decks later, the count went up once again. I stood up from the table again uttering something about "being nervous." I gave signals from the rail, letting Allen play far more $500 hands than if I'd stayed at the table.

At the end of the pack, I gave the "end-of-session" signal to Allen. As Allen got up to leave, the boss came over to us, the spectator gallery, and said, "Sorry, folks. The show's over."

Either Glynn or I put on this same type of play with Allen at the Hacienda. We played day and graveyard shifts over and over again with no problem. Swing shift, on the other hand, shuffled on Allen his first night, so we stayed out of there between six P.M. and two A.M.

*When a counter runs into unfavorable, negative counts, he can spread horizontally, that is, make two, three or more small bets of, say, $25. This tends to "eat up" the cards, and force the shuffle of the negative deck sooner.

By having Allen play alone in positive counts, we were doing the reverse, in effect "card-conserving," so the BP would get more rounds in favorable situations.

I discovered, first-hand, that it was a mistake to put down "advance cover" against an inexperienced pit boss.

The Riviera had opened several $200-limit blackjack games in their separate mini-casino.

Neil and I walked in. I decided to have Neil throw out a little cover, to "get established." I found a game with good penetration and called Neil in, signaling him a $200 bet off the top. The count went up. The female floorperson seemed to be watching the cards, and I suspected she might have been counting. I cut Neil's next bet to $50. He won. The count was up there, but I kept the third bet at $50. The floorperson whispered something to the dealer. The dealer shuffled.

Neil came out with $200 off the top. He won the bet, but the count dropped. I maintained his bet at $200 for the next two hands. Once again, after the third round, the dealer shuffled.

There was no correlation between Neil's betting and the count; in fact, his big bets were off the top, or when the count was negative, and vice versa.

On one hand, Neil asked the floorperson what she thought he should bet. She shrugged, "Bet anything you want."

"Should I bet $200?"

Neil was trying to "lay down some cover," by leaving the decision totally with the boss, as if he, the hunch gambler, couldn't have cared less. This didn't impress her. She shrugged again, "It's OK with me."

He bet $200.

The apparent arbitrary betting scheme didn't work. The dealer kept on shuffling.

Neil finally asked the boss, "Why all the shuffling?"

She replied, "Any time I see variation like that, I shuffle."

We'd outsmarted ourselves.

Our large bank size gave us a flexibility we didn't have before. It allowed us to bet much bigger off the top, particularly when we had a dead-even bet, at clubs like Circus Circus and the Landmark, which offered single-deck games with Strip rules.

Betting $500 or $1,000 off the top, on average, doesn't cost the team a dime. However, it can cause huge fluctuations in bankroll. (It is a mathematical fact that fluctuations increase as the player's edge drops.) With our $125,000 (which had grown to $140,000 on our second day in town), we could bet much larger off the top, and thus keep the heat off our players.

Off-the-top betting, in my opinion, is not exploited nearly enough by most counters or teams. For some reason, the average counter would rather be caught dead than be stuck with a big bet out in a negative deck. This can often be false economy.

If a small sacrifice (say, the $5 that a $1,000 bet costs with a .5% disadvantage) can create thousands of dollars of earnings potential, it's obviously a good investment.

Even the casinos are starting to understand this concept. In a craps game, casinos offer "double odds," "triple odds," or, in some clubs, such as Benny Binion's Horseshoe, "ten times odds."*

The casinos don't make a dime on the odds bets; they're dead-even propositions, just like flipping a (fair) coin. But the clubs are willing to put up with these profitless bets to generate additional profitable play. Our team was using this same philosophy.

Circus usually doesn't have good penetration. However, when there's a full table, with seven players, about 43 cards out of the 52, on average, are dealt.

I played Circus by myself, with no BP and no disguise. They knew me as a "legitimate" high-roller.

We used off-the-top betting, combined with multiple hands, to get the bosses used to erratic, and seemingly harmless, bet variation. I remember one series of plays, with two players and myself at the table (and a short, rotund boss we nicknamed "Beachball" closely hawking the game), that went something like this:

| | | |
|---|---|---|
| Shuffle | 1 Hand—Bet $200 (2 blacks) | Win |
| Count Up | 1 Hand—Bet $175 (1 black, 3 green) | Lose |
| Count down | 2 Hands—$100; $50 | Win |

*Benny's club has always allowed huge maximum bets, up to $10,000 per hand and higher. They once allowed a player to bet $777,000 on one play of the dice. He won. A few years later that same bettor returned and bet $1,000,000 on one craps play. This time, the player lost. Shortly thereafter, he committed suicide; the media claimed his demise was due to an unhappy romance, not to the million bucks he lost.

Benny once allowed me to play a $50,000 challenge match on national TV, hosted by David Hartman. David interviewed Benny and asked him why he allowed higher stakes play in his casino than the fancy casinos on the Strip. Benny replied, "Well they got the big clubs with the little bankrolls. I got a little club with a big bankroll."

| | | |
|---|---|---|
| Shuffle | 1 Hand—$450 | Win |
| Count Down | 2 Hands—$200; $150 | Split |
| Count Down | 3 Hands—$125; $85; 105 | Split |
| | | |
| Shuffle | 1 Hand $5 | Lose |
| Count Down | 2 Hands—$50; $60 | Split |
| Count Down | 3 Hands—$100; $75; $50 (Dealer Shuffles—not enough cards) | No Hand |
| | | |
| Shuffle | Combine above 3 bets to $225 | Lose |
| Count Up | $430 | Win |
| Count Up | $410 | Win |
| Count Up | $375 | Lose |
| | | |
| Shuffle | $500 | Lose |
| Count Up | 2 Hands (Steaming) $500 and $275 | Win |
| Count Up | $500 (Regaining sense and pulling back) | Lose |
| | | |
| Shuffle | $375 | Lose |
| Count Down | 3 Hands—$100; 60; 35 | Split |
| And so on. | | |

After 20 minutes of this, Beachball walked away; there was a subtle pattern, and the bets were generally moving with the count. But the "violations" were so crass that the more subtle movements were undectable even by a counting boss, to say nothing of the boss who doesn't count. (Most bosses, I find, don't really count, but simply look for concentrations of high cards and aces—or low cards—on the spread or in the discard pile.)

I would make the "violation" bets even more crass when the count moved down obviously (absurd amounts of "paint" on the table) or up obviously (many little cards on the table.)

When the boss leaves, we can now vary bets, with the count, to our heart's content. When he returns, we revert to the original, erratic pattern (sneaking in some good stuff once in a while).

And it often gets even better. Because, as I said, once a player is "established" by the pit, the dealers are aware of this and often relax and give him far greater penetration than before.

Landmark: I put out $300. I get caught; the dealer shuffles.

Boss turns to dealer to corroborate the dealer's decision: "Whenever he puts out $300 . . ."

I quickly cap the $300 with two more blacks, making $500.

Dealer: "What?"

Boss: "Never mind."

By accident, I found out how valuable Caesar's white ($500) chips were—for a different reason.

I sat down at a table at the Mint, on a totally impromptu play, after a session at Caesars. I had only $700 in cash, but also had $3,000 in Caesars chips.

The Mint bosses carefully watched their single-deck games, which often had good penetration. I started to play with my limited cash. I lost $400, reached in my pocket, and threw the $3,000 in Caesars chips on the table, saying "Can I use these if I get stuck?"

One boss went to the podium. He returned in two minutes and said, "We'll take 'em, if you want."

A second boss immediately came over, gave me his card, and said, "We're not Caesars, but you're welcome to anything we have here."

Both bosses ignored the game. I sensed they were thinking something along the lines of, "This guy's a Caesars high-roller. We'll show him we have class, too, just like Caesars, and not sweat the game just because he's betting high."

The same night I did the same thing at the Horseshoe. They were happy to agree to cash the chips. After the play, they sent me back to Caesars in their limousine. (Then I took a cab to the apartment.)

The following day, I tried the same ploy at the Lady Luck casino in downtown Vegas—definitely not what you'd call a high-roller casino. Once again, the Caesars chips seemed to intimidate the pit.

The bosses were even more apologetic, friendly, and, most importantly, didn't watch the game. In this case, I sensed they were thinking, "The guy's a Caesars customer, 'slumming.' We can't begin to expect to have him as a steady customer, but let's be thankful he's giving us some action."

The Caesars chips worked their magic on the Strip, too, at the Hacienda, Flamingo Hilton and Imperial Palace.

The boys were doing well. Within a few days, Glynn, Allen, and I were each up over five figures. I'd like to have been able to attribute this to our new techniques, but I knew better.

There was no doubt that we were playing stronger, with our counter-counter and on-the-rail approaches. But random fluctuations, I felt, were more predominant than the increase in our edge that we'd produced.

Neil joked, "Maybe it was karma," referring to what we felt was our creativity, hard work, and persistence.

At any rate, things were looking good. We had minimal heat in town, and our new techniques seemed virtually undetectable.

# 16

# An Early Court Skirmish

It was time to put on the suit again for a nine A.M. hearing. Why do they always schedule these things in the middle of the night? It was still graveyard (two A.M.-ten A.M.) shift, for Chrissakes.

When I got to the courthouse, four opposition lawyers were there—the Deputy Attorney General, his assistant, and two lawyers for the Nevada Resort Association.

Judge Thompson entered. "Hear ye, hear ye." Everybody rose.

The judge was a young, clean-cut, chin-to-the-wind type. He briskly cleared up a few legal matters. It was obvious he was articulate, decisive, and efficient.

He also struck me as being ambitious—probably not content to remain a District Court judge all his life. He probably wanted to move up in the judicial hierarchy, maybe even someday be Governor.

I took this as a plus factor. The logic went like this:

1. Ambitious, young judges don't want to be overturned—it's a blot on their record.

2. This judge knew I was litigious; by now, he'd read documents

revealing that I'd been in several Nevada courts and all the way up to the Jersey Supreme Court.

3. Thus, he may review this case on its merits.

On the other hand, you could look at it like this:

1. Ambitious, young judges make friends in high places.

2. The Attorney General is in a high place; so is the Chairman of the Commission.

3. So's the President of Caesar's Palace, the Golden Nugget, and the MGM.

4. Uston, go home.

Our case was called. The Judge asked the Deputy Attorney General why he should dismiss the petition. The lawyer argued separation of powers.

"Uston asked for a rule change, which is a legislative, not a judicial, matter"

The judge cut in: "You mean I don't have jurisdiction to review this?"

I liked it. It sounded like they were telling the judge it was none of his business, and the judge didn't like it.

The Attorney General finished up.

Then it was my turn.

"Your Honor, the Attorney General maintains that this Court may review only Commission decisions involving disciplinary action. Yet there are five judicial review sections which are phrased much more broadly, and refer virtually to any decision made by the Commission."

At least the judge was listening.

He became more attentive, when I said, "Not only that, Your Honor, but there's one section that not only covers judicial review, but is addressed specifically to judicial remedy at the next level—with the Supreme Court in Carson City.

"Certainly Supreme Court remedies aren't restricted solely to disciplinary actions. In fact, the statutes say they apply to 'any person aggrieved by action of Commission.'

"And I was certainly aggrieved at the June 20 hearing."

I had more to say, but the judge cut me off:

"I'll take the matter under advisement."

End of subject. We all picked up our papers and filed out of the courtroom.

I went across the street and played lawyer-gambler at the Horseshoe. The game was good, but I lost $3,300. I won $2,100 of it back, at the Mint.

The judge's "advisement" was to last over two months.

# 17

# Some More New Approaches

## First-Basing

I was walking through the MGM, during day shift, wearing the wig, baseball cap, and eyeglasses. I spotted a dealer who exposed his hole card from first base when he checked for blackjack. (MGM dealers still followed the traditional policy of looking at the holecard when they had a ten or ace upcard.) The "first-baser" was about 60, partially bald, and had gray hair and a paunch. His name was "Doc."

When checking for blackjack, Doc picked up his holecard with his right hand in a way that allowed a player standing at first base to look over the top of Doc's left hand and see the upper left-hand index.

I decided to put on a holecard play, the first I'd done in years.

Holecarding has always been controversial. Years ago, we had no idea whether it was legal or not; there'd never been a legal decision.

A few years ago, one of my ex-teammates was caught at Circus Circus playing a front-loader. The bosses caught onto the play and called the police. The cops arrested both the player and the dealer on the spot and paraded them out of the casino in handcuffs, for all the patrons to see.

The two men were suspected of being in collusion. When it was proved that they didn't know each other, the judge dismissed the charges, saying, "If the dealer shows the card, the player has a right to look at it."

More recently, two players were caught playing holecards and were arrested. It appeared that one player was spotting the holecard, and signaling to a second player, a BP, who played the big money.

Both players were acquitted in court. The state appealed to the Nevada Supreme Court—they wanted to set an example with these guys. But the players were once again found innocent of any cheating. The Supreme Court in effect ruled that holecard play, such as front-loading and first-basing, was not illegal.

(It would be interesting to know if the decision would have been different, if these players had been "spooking"—with one of the men standing *behind* the dealer and signaling holecard information across the pit to the player.)

By acquitting these players, the top court in Nevada had sanctioned team holecard play, signals and all (Sheriff vs. Einbinder and Dalben, Nevada Supreme Court #157997, filed December, 1984).

It is far better to have more than one person at the table when spotting holecards—that is, one player, betting small, who's reading the card, and a second player betting the big money. The bosses are far more likely to pick up on the play if a high-roller is at a location from which the holecard can be seen. But if the BP sits in an "innocent" position and never looks anywhere near the dealer when the dealer checks his holecard, the bosses are often totally bamboozled.

At the beginning of day shift on the following day, a Friday, I went back to the MGM, looking for Doc. If I found him, I planned to phone Rambo, who could come over and be the BP.

Doc was nowhere to be found.

He also had a day off on Saturday. On Sunday, I finally saw him dealing at a $5 table. I watched for a while; Doc was still "readable." I went to the phone and summoned Rambo. I said, "Bring 15 grand, we may be chunking."

When I returned to Doc's table, I was dismayed to see that a lady sat down at first base; she was playing nickels. The lady had several hundred dollars in chips in front of her, so it seemed as if she planned on staying a while. It didn't look good. I stood next to her and watched the game. Suddenly, I realized that by moving slightly to the right when Doc checked his holecard, I could see its value.

I started chatting with the lady. Fortunately, she was friendly and was delighted to have me stand next to her and watch her play. Her name was Doris; she was from Phoenix. We chatted about restaurants in Phoenix and Scottsdale, the Arizona desert, the Camelback Inn, the way her cards were running, and just about anything else I could think of.

Rambo showed up. I put my hand on my cheek, signaling him to sit down. Rambo sat down about halfway between the middle spot and third base. Perfect.

With a first-baser, even without counting, the player has an edge of close to 2%, if he sees the holecard every time it's checked (which is 5 out of 13, or 38% of the time.) Since we were counting, our edge was even higher. With our bank size, we could bet well over $1,000 per hand. I decided to start conservatively, however. Doc was the first holecarder I'd played in years, and I didn't know holecard Basic Strategy perfectly.*

Rambo and I had tailor-made a set of betting signals for this play, since with holecard play we bet much higher. Since we'd assumed I'd be playing at the table, they were chip betting signals. Obviously I would now have to use our conventional on-the-rail signals, which we hadn't modified for this play.

Rambo cashed in for $2,000. I scratched the top of my head. Rambo put out $500.

The dealer had a 9 up—no holecard to check. I played the conventional count.

After several deals, Doc had a ten up. I saw his king in the hole. Neil had a 17. There was nothing I could do. Obviously Rambo should have hit, but hitting hard 17's is a quick way to get thrown out for hole-carding. We stood on the hand, and ate the loss (in the past, we'd occasionally gotten away with hitting three- or four-card 17's

*Computer runs had identified some surprising holecard Basic Strategy plays, which the holecard player had to memorize. For example, we had to split 2's, 3's, 7's, 8's, and 9's, versus a dealer's 18; split 9's against a 19; and double down on 9, 10, 11, A,6, and A,7 versus a dealer A,5.

against a "pat"; if the dealer remarked about it, we pretended that we'd added our cards up incorrectly).

Two bosses were watching Rambo. They didn't even look at me. The count was sky high. I signaled "super-chunk." Rambo bet $1,000. Rambo drew a twenty; Doc had a 10 up. Doc checked his holecard; it was a 4.

Now splitting 10's against a 10 is usually a stupid play. When you're holecarding, you get the feeling that everyone in the world will guess what you're doing if you pull plays like this. I suspect in many cases this is paranoia.

If the holecard player doesn't make these plays, much of the extra edge is lost. Since the MGM was a club that, were it not for holecards, we would never play, I decided to go for the gusto. I put my thumb up, and Rambo split.

Rambo drew a 6 and a 7.

Doris gasped and whispered to me,

"Some people have more money than brains."

I agreed, "The guy's nuts."

Doc turned over his holecard. I was relieved that it was a 4, because it *is* possible to read holecards incorrectly.

Doc drew a ten and busted. Another two thousand bucks!

When it goes well, holecarding's great. There's an incredible feeling of power, when the dealer keeps getting stiffs and you know it in advance and capitalize on it. When the dealer is pat, say with a 20, you often save lots of money by avoiding such plays as doubling on 11 or splitting aces and eights.

There are times when the holecard always seems to work against the player—as when you stand on 13 because the dealer has a stiff, and he makes his hand with the 7 or 8 that you would have drawn had you not known the value of his holecard. Yes, there are still plenty of black beans in that jar when playing holecards (even a huge 4% edge is equivalent to only 52 white beans versus 48 black ones). It's all part of the game.

Suddenly I noticed the feral boss approaching (the boss who'd given me the one-round-and-shuffle routine about a month before) and froze. Although he was working in another pit, he came over to check out Rambo. I stepped back from Doris's chair, and kept my head lowered, as if I'd been watching only Doris's play; my eyes were shielded from him by the visor on the baseball cap.

I stroked my forehead with the back of my wrist (the "heat" signal) and hoped Rambo got the message: "Cut the bets, and play basic strategy."

Several rounds went by. Finally my Feral Friend left. I'd lost the count. Doc drew no ten or ace upcards for the rest of the shoe. I left Rambo to his own devices until after the shuffle.

Doc went on break, and I called the absurdly unprofitable MGM game the best I could. The count for the relief dealer's first shoe went way down, and I reduced Rambo's bets as rapidly as I dared. (The bosses may get suspicious if a player bets big against one dealer and bets small against his relief.)

We were making a lot of black chip bets into negative shoes. I didn't want to give Rambo a "break signal" (too obvious), and yet I didn't want him to radically lower his bets with Doc on break.

One shoe went positive, and I signaled $500. The cutcard came up so quickly that we got off only two big bets before the shuffle. Now I was worried that Rambo's variation would "make" him as a counter. I signaled more cover bets. At that point I wondered if I was giving away, mathematically, as much as we were gaining. Finally Doc returned.

Doc continued to be 100% readable. Rambo was flat-betting $1,000 a hand. Then there was a long, dry spell. For hand after hand, Doc didn't get either a ten or ace upcard. When this happens, there's a tendency to get frustrated, anxiously waiting for "the action."

However, even under these conditions the holecard player is in good shape. The dealer is drawing nothing but 2 through 9 upcards; thus in many cases the counter maintains a comfortable edge over the house.

Doc's 45-minute stint was over. Rambo was up a little over $10,000. When Doc took his next break, I called off the play.

The bosses stood for Rambo's action, but they apparently didn't like it. Rambo was betting as high as anyone in the entire place, and they didn't even offer him a ham sandwich.

## Modified Team Play

We had a chance to experiment with a variation of the old team approach used by the first team I'd ever played with. You'll recall that we stationed counters at four or five tables. The counters were novices; they knew how to count shoes, but didn't know the matrix numbers or how to make betting calculations.

They would count down the shoe and signal the BP when the decks became "hot." When the BP came to the table, the counter signaled the running count and the number of aces played. The BP took it from there.

We had to do it differently. Our counters were the experts, and our "gorilla BP's" knew nothing about counting. Our plan: the BP's would still "bop" from table-to-table, but the counters would signal all the bets and the plays for the BP.

We conducted a trial-run at the $200-maximum Bourbon Street Casino. This club had excellent penetration. They usually dealt 3½ decks or more, out of 4 decks, and they allowed the player to double down on split pairs. Since it was a newer—and smaller—club, we'd hoped that their bosses might be inexperienced or perhaps less competent castoffs from some of the better clubs in town.

Allen, Glynn, and I took Rambo to Bourbon Street.

At first the bosses were wary about Rambo, who was running around from table to table, betting one, two or three hands of $200. But good old Rambo started throwing down double Scotches by the wagonful, and before long, the bosses were laughing and joking with him.

Allen and Glynn were counting at two tables on one side of the pit; I was on the other side. We had Rambo bopping all over the casino.

Bourbon Street was fairly empty. This made the play even more efficient because Glynn, Allen and I could change tables when our shoe went "irrevocably" cold. We found an empty table and "cracked" another shoe.

I watched as Allen and Glynn leap-frogged tables on the other side of the pit. It was hilarious. After Rambo joined them, if some other counter wasn't "hot," he stayed at the table, betting smaller, until that shoe, or another one, became "hot."

Most of the tables didn't have black chips. It was becoming impossible for Rambo to carry his chips from table to table without dropping them. He pulled his shirt out of his pants and carried the chips there. Finally he asked for a rack. Before long, Rambo needed a second rack. The dealers were getting a kick out of this guy running around with his own racks of chips, apparently betting randomly at virtually all the tables.

Rambo finally alighted on a table that had black chips. To solve his logistics problem, he put a rack of greens on the table and said "Black chips, please."

The dealer announced, "Massive change of color."

Unfortunately, Rambo didn't have the problem of carrying chips around the casino for long. He started losing bet after bet. It seemed that we counters drew nothing but 20's and blackjacks; all Rambo could pull were 13's, 14's, 15's, and 16's.

Rambo was soon into cash again. The play went well technically. However, when I finally called it, Rambo was down $3,100.

Rambo remained in the casino, talking to one of the bosses, an older man who had offered him a comp. Rambo went into the gift shop and returned with a huge stuffed animal. He gave it to the boss.

When we got back to the apartment, I asked Rambo, "That boss likes stuffed animals? I don't believe it."

Rambo said, "No. He just kept talking about his grandson. When I gave him the bear, he was pleased as punch."

"You sly sonavagun."

A few days after our first-basing play, Allen went into the MGM. He couldn't read Doc. Then Glynn tried—in vain.

I complained to them, "Do I have to do everything around here?"

The following day I returned to the MGM. This was a risky move. Wig or not, it didn't make a lot of sense for me to be seen in the vicinity of first base at Doc's table with Rambo—or anybody else—high-rolling there.

I wasn't as great as I thought I was. Doc had indeed tightened up. Did the bosses realize what was going on and correct him?

We'll never know.

We stayed in Vegas, using counter-counter and on-the-rail play at the double-deck games at the Trop, Sundance, Dunes, Imperial Palace, and Riviera. Once in a while I played on my own.

Periodically, we put down a modified team play at a four-deck club, concentrating on Bourbon Street and the El Rancho; once we even went back into the heat-laden Sands on graveyard shift. Team play was fun, but it was also inefficient: We had to use all our counters to get down just one play.

Our bank was now over $200,000, and we had won well beyond "expected value"; but considering the losses from the first effort, we were probably, mathematically, just about on target.

## Uston Wigs Out

On one of the very last plays before I left town, I did something really stupid. Periodically, I played Caesars' four-deck games on my own. Many dealers dealt 3 ½ out of four decks, and the player had the surrender and double-on-split options. This was definitely the best four-deck game in town—or in the country, for that matter.

Caesars had only four four-deck games. The games are lined up, down the center aisle of the main casino. These tables generally had $25 minimums. On week-ends, the minimums were often raised to $50 or $100.

I was playing, with my wig and glasses, totally unnoticed at one game. At the very next table was a private game for a Korean gentleman I'll call Mr. Chu. Mr. Chu was betting yellow ($1,000) chips. He bet from three hands of $5,000 to six hands of $5,000. He had about $125,000 in yellow chips on the table.

With Caesars' double-on-split rule, the player can find the amount bet suddenly quadrupled, or more. If Mr. Chu doubled on both split pairs on one of his $5,000 bets, his bet, on just that one square, would suddenly escalate to $20,000.

On many occasions, Mr. Chu had $40,000 (or more) on the betting squares. Thus a single card drawn by the dealer could determine whether he won or lost $40,000—an $80,000 swing in Mr. Chu's net worth.

Mr. Chu had an entourage of half a dozen men. One of them was playing black chips at my table. He frequently looked over to see how Mr. Chu was doing, as did most of the players at my table.

On one particularly dramatic hand, I stood up to watch Mr. Chu. Just as I rose, a boss from the other side of the pit glanced over at me. He looked away and quickly looked back. Then he nodded his head and smiled.

He started to walk over to my table. I couldn't believe it. Because of dumb curiosity, I had blown my new disguise in one of the best clubs in town.

If I'd just kept my head down, minded my own business, played my four-hour shift and gotten out of there, everything would have been fine.

"Kenny, I almost didn't recognize you."

I said, meekly, "How ya' doin?"

He laughed. "Where's your cane and your seeing-eye dog?"

"I'm just fooling around. Nothing serious."

He said, "Have fun, Kenny," and walked away.

I watched him as he walked to the other side of the pit, and whispered to another one of the bosses.

I took off, hoping to prevent pictures from the sky that would blow me out on the other two shifts.

The smallest mistake can cost a lot of money.

# 18

# I Go to Law School

After playing two straight weeks, I was burned out with Vegas and went back to San Francisco to forget about ace adjustment, pit bosses, and 16's against a 10. The team stayed in Vegas.

It was November 15, 1985, a day I'll never forget. I still can't believe it!

I was having a pop down at my local watering hole, The Washington Square Bar and Grill, when I was paged. I grabbed the phone. It was Inga.

"Kenny. They're going to hear your case!"

"What?"

"Robert called. It's in the papers in Vegas. The judge ruled in your favor." I was incredulous. Judge Thompson denied the Attorney General's Motion To Dismiss!

We beat the Attorney General of Nevada—in Nevada!

I thought, "Even if it's the only decision I ever win, we won one. There *is* some justice."

I hung up and immediately telephoned Walt Tyminski of *Rouge Et Noir*. Walt said, "Ken, that was to be expected. They had to do it. If they didn't agree to hear your case, they knew you could challenge the whole thing on grounds of constitutionality."

Walt went on, "You should subpoena them."

"Who?"

"The ones who insisted you go for a rule change."

He was referring to James Avance, the Former Board Chairman who left that job to become a bigwig in the Bourbon Street Casino.

Walt had a point. Now that the case was definitely going to be heard, perhaps we could capitalize on the power of subpoena.

What made the day even better was that, an hour later, Inga got another call from Vegas.

Allen and Glynn had won $21,000 during the previous two days.

Inga and I celebrated well into the night. What an upper! It was hard to believe—a positive court decision in the State of Nevada!

We kept asking, "Why?"

We concluded it was for one of three reasons:

—Judge Thompson felt the pressure from the good 'ol boys to keep the Feds out, concerned that if he didn't allow the case to be heard, I'd go to Federal Court.

—The Nevada establishment assumed that they could kill me in court anyway, so why bother ducking the issue.

—It was an honest, objective decision; it's what the judge really felt.

What do you think?

I kept repeating: "A judge ruled in our favor in Nevada! A judge ruled in our favor in Nevada! A judge ruled in our favor in Nevada!"

I had to pinch myself to really believe it.

### Down to Earth

Three days later, Glen Alberich, one of the lawyers who handled the New Jersey case, called from Boston. He had a lot to say that made me feel I couldn't handle this myself.

"Ken, there are essential legal issues involved here, in what will end up being a summary judgment.

"It's tough to argue these points in a winnable way. There are statutory construction arguments and statutory policy arguments.

"There's a precedent case for everything. The point is to differentiate the germane ones, and to come up with a reasonable public policy.

"If you lose based on arguments of law, it will be real tough—probably impossible—to overcome at a higher level.

"The judge needs analysis and supporting public policy. You'll be fighting the big guns in Nevada. They'll offer him nine or ten reasons for supporting their side. They'll consider the tax structure, school systems, employment of people, you name it.

"Thus you've got to balance the issue versus general public policies—and come up with a rational scheme for all that."

I didn't understand half of what Glen was saying, let alone thinking I could write a brief around it.

But I got the point. Was I kidding myself to think I could possibly do this myself? The alternative was to incur absurd legal fees.

What to do?

The next day, I called the Nevada ACLU. A lawyer there seemed interested, but said the Nevada ACLU had no funds to help out. He gave me the number of a Vegas law professor, whom I'll call Bill, who was an expert in gaming law.

I called Bill and told him the problem. He said, "I'll help you—call it a labor of love."

Perhaps this would be a real break. Within hours, I Fed Ex'd to Bill a copy of the entire file.

## An Attempt to Introduce More Evidence

December 6, 1985. Today I took a close look at the Nevada statutes. One statute allowed new evidence to be introduced if it was "material and necessary and sufficient reason existed for failure to present the evidence at the hearing."

It seemed as if I might be able to introduce additional evidence to the Commission. (It couldn't be submitted to the court, which could only consider evidence in the Commission record.)

For starters, lawyer-friend Les Combs had come to the hearing to testify on behalf of card-counters who were barred, photographed, arrested, and sometimes physically assaulted. He came to the hearing at 10:30 A.M., but had to leave at one P.M. to catch a plane. Our case wasn't called until 3:40 P.M.

Secondly, the Horseshoe beatings of Allen Brown and Barry Finn happened five months after the hearing. I thought they'd certainly be "material." Brown almost died as a result of card-counting (he and his friend were also first-basing). This incident could not have been introduced at the hearing—it hadn't happened yet. I hoped that the judge would admit events that occurred after the Commission hearings.

As I reviewed the letters sent me by the Commission, it struck me that the June 20 hearing was called to discuss whether the Commission would *proceed* with consideration of my petition, not to rule on the petition itself. The transcript reinforces this, quoting me as saying:

". . . as I understand the hearing today, WE ARE NOT CONSIDERING THE CHANGE PER SE, but rather considering whether the commission will consider the issue."

I prepared a Motion To Introduce Additional Evidence, stating:

"Petitioner was notified that procedural matters would be discussed. He so prepared himself. The petition itself was denied without Petitioner having the opportunity to assemble and present all of the facts supporting the petition."

I asked for the right to introduce additional testimony or affidavits. I had a feeling that the Attorney General and NRA would hit the ceiling when they read that I wanted to introduce evidence from:

1. Les Combs, the lawyer who represented several counters in lawsuits with casinos. Les could testify that counters have not only been barred, but detained in back rooms, photographed against their will, put in the Griffin Mug Book, arrested by the cops, and beaten up.

2. The four pit bosses who barred me in Tahoe and a couple of friends who witnessed the barrings.

3. Pit bosses who barred counters and who knew ways to offset the edge of counters. I thought I might be able to trap the bosses into supporting our cause:

—If they testified that they barred counters, that would help to establish that fact.

—If they denied that they barred counters, the obvious follow-up question would be, "Then what do you do?"

If they replied, "Shuffle up" or, "Move the cut card forward," they were implying that the card-counter edge can be overcome by simple counter-measures.

4. Allen Brown and Barry Finn, to discuss their beatings, and also their doctors and the Horseshoe security guards who beat them up.

5. Griffin and his agents, to testify about the Mug Book and other "counter-fliers" they circulate to the casinos. I also asked for a copy of the Mug Book.

6. The casino bigwigs who told the Jersey Commission that they'd discontinue blackjack if they had to admit counters. It was all applesauce, but I expected to hear the same tired testimony in Nevada from the NRA.

7. James Avance, the Chairman of the Gaming Control Board, who led me to file for a rule change instead of granting me a hearing. I was concerned, as Walt Tyminski pointed out, that I might lose the case because of that technicality.

I wanted to show the Court that I didn't care about a rule change. All I wanted was for casinos to be prevented from throwing me (and other counters) out.

It would also be interesting if Avance knew about his Bourbon Street Casino job when he ruled on my petition.

Bill, the law professor, called. He told me he'd spent an entire morning reading the file. So, he said, had Glen:

"The case is a matter of law, period."

I knew it was Law, and not Chemical Engineering or Nuclear Physics. I had to find out what that statement meant—and why it seemed so important to everyone.

Bill thought that Glen's Jersey briefs were excellent, but that my petition was poorly done. He said, "You mixed legal arguments with allegations," whatever that meant.

Again, I didn't understand most of what Bill was saying, but I wrote it all down for future reference. Bill endorsed the idea of filing the motion for more evidence: "No harm in asking."

He emphasized, "You must get an extension of time. That's number one."

I was glad Bill was helping. He seemed to know his stuff and was obviously quite interested in the case.

And Bill talked logically. He didn't use a lot of the legalese gobbledegook that so many lawyers seem to prefer.

I finished the Motion for Additional Evidence and, at Bill's suggestion, requested a 30-day extension of the December 18, 1985, due date for the filing of my brief.

This legal stuff gets complicated. After talking to the Court Clerk in Vegas, I discovered that something called a "Notice of Motion" had to be prepared. Also a "Proof of Service." I pulled out the Attorney General's Motion To Dismiss and copied the format for each.

December 10. I mailed the papers to Vegas and to the opposition. Also, for the first time, I studied the NRA's Motion To Dismiss in detail.

I thought the NRA's motion was persuasive. After reading their arguments, I felt real lucky that the judge had ruled in our favor.

Then I wondered why the judge had denied their motion. Was he intrigued with this rather unusual case? Did he want to hear the case because of its widespread implications? Could it have been the publicity? (That was a cynical thought! Surely, all judges are strictly objective and don't concern themselves with such mundane matters as publicity.)

December 13. Bad news. The judge announced that he would allow no more extensions. He scheduled my Motion for Additional Evidence for hearing on January 8.

Today is Friday. I had four-plus to prepare the Opening Brief.

I suspected that this augured poorly for our side. I had no idea what research had to be done, or how time-consuming it would be to prepare a brief. I'd never prepared a brief. (I had a copy of the New Jersey brief and planned to copy that format.)

December 17. After 4½ straight 16-hour days, I finished the Opening Brief. I felt good about it. But then, I suspect that every lawyer feels optimistic after he's shed blood, sweat and tears researching, organizing, writing, rewriting, and re-rewriting a brief. This one, with exhibits, was over 50 pages long.

Finally I studied the cases cited by the opposition. Lawyer-friend Nancy took me to a San Francisco law library and showed me how to look up cases. Would you believe—all that gobbledegook is really quite logical.

For example, if a citation read:

"Uston v. Resorts International Hotel, 431 A.2nd 173," that designated the name of the case and where the decision could be found; in this case, in volume 431, of a legal series called Atlantic 2nd Supplement, page 173. It was that easy.

I also found something that Bill told me to be totally true. He'd advised:

"Look up all the opposition's cases. Chances are, you'll find they really don't apply—and sometimes you can use these cases to your own advantage."

That precise thing happened. The NRA had cited seven cases in which racetracks had ejected patrons (the implication: that therefore casinos could eject card-counters). Of the seven, four involved exclusions of undesirable characters, one involved civil rights issues, which were not at issue here, and two involved states (Arizona and New Hampshire) that had laws giving the racetracks "sole judgment" in ejecting people.

It just goes to show you—you have to watch lawyers.

I filed the brief, sent out copies, and mailed requests for affidavits from friendly witnesses. Then I went out for a few vodka-grapefruits.

I had mixed feelings about the case.

I was elated because I'd just completed a complicated project, one I hadn't been sure I could handle. For the first time, I felt that I had the edge in this battle. If I were forced to put $10,000 on winning or losing at this point, I would have bet on winning. After the exhaustive research, I felt that the Nevada law supported our case. Of course, I hadn't received the opposition's reply, which might totally dispel this feeling of optimism.

On the other hand, I wondered if I was really doing the right thing. Just about every interest I could think of wanted me to lose this case, for different reasons.

—The Nevada casinos wanted the right to bar counters.

—The NRA wanted what the casinos wanted.

—The Commission was the opposition.

—The Nevada Attorney General was not only the opposing counsel, but I suspected their lawyers would feel humiliated if some guy who wasn't even a lawyer beat them in court.

—The Griffin Agency would lose business if they couldn't list card-counters in their Mug Book and circulate fliers to their casino clients.

—Card-counters were worried that, if I won, the game of blackjack would be ruined. (I thought that competition between casinos would probably keep the game beatable.)

—Blackjack authors and teachers would fear that the game would become unbeatable and thus they'd be put out of business.

—Les Combs and other lawyers would lose business if counters were no longer hassled by casinos.

—Me. If the game were altered, our team might be out of business. It would also endanger the royalties from my blackjack books, video cassette, and computer software that instructed people how to play blackjack. I also couldn't help wondering if I might not be risking physical violence, something friends would occasionally suggest.

I tried to imagine who might want me to win:

—Perhaps the few Atlantic City casinos which had no Nevada operations—Resorts, Trump and Atlantis. (Ironically, Resorts was the New Jersey casino that I beat in court.)

—People who teach those controversial systems which supposedly show people how to win at blackjack without counting, like Doug Grant.

—The general public. But do they really care?

—The media. They benefit by reporting on controversy.

Nevertheless, I knew that I would continue to pursue my case.

First, I'd done too much work to quit now.

Second, I enjoyed the work. It was intriguing to do legal research and to lock horns with, and try to out-strategize and out-think, a bunch of high-priced attorneys. Working on this case was like trying to solve a puzzle, trying to find the right pieces (i.e., precedents and Nevada statutes) and putting them together in a logical, persuasive way.

It was an adventure, which was full of irony. Here we were, fighting the casinos on two fronts simultaneously, at the tables and in the courts.

There was obviously another reason—ego. If I won at District Court, the NRA would certainly appeal to the Supreme Court.

If I lost, I'd appeal (I had looked into the appeal process; it didn't seem that complicated).

How many guys get to argue before a Supreme Court, representing themselves?

A lot of lawyers never get the chance. And the ones who do, think it's a big deal. When we were in the New Jersey Supreme Court, the opposing lawyer dressed up his family and brought them to court to watch his star performance. So he was clearly proud—and this was a big-time Trenton lawyer who was once counsel for the Governor of New Jersey!

The final reason, which sounds like motherhood and apple pie, was that I didn't doubt for an instant that we were right. I felt strongly about this cause. I'd been working for it off and on for ten years.

I had yet to talk to anyone who thought it was right for casinos to arbitrarily bar good players. And I've talked to hundreds of people about this: cab drivers, lawyers, actors, waiters, and talk show hosts—even casino executives (off the record, of course).

# 19

# More Heat in Vegas

The entire team was in Vegas once again. Allen and Inga had just returned from a short but fabulous session.

Allen took Inga to Caesars. In 15 minutes, they won $3,100 and left. No one even knew they were there.

They crossed the street and went to the Dunes. They won $2,250 in five minutes—literally. Out the door.

They went to the Sahara and won $1,750 in 10 minutes. A little heat started simmering, but they had cashed out before the bosses could even react.

Allen and Inga came back to the apartment. Total elapsed time: 1 ½ hours. Total win: $7,100.

Allen exuded confidence, as if he deserved the win. It's funny how the mindset of a counter works. When things are going really well and you can't lose a hand, you begin to feel invincible. The double downs work the way they're supposed to. When the count is high and you have a big bet out, the dealer has a 6 up and a 10 in the hole and hits with another 10, just like the book says.

You feel you deserve those results. That's the way the world is. There *is* some justice. The game is easy. There's no better way to make a living. How could I ever do anything else?

And it often happens that when we win, we work less. We're turning over 19's, 20's, and blackjacks, and not making the tiring calculations that come with 15's against a 10, 16's against a 9, and other stiffs. It's also been our experience that less heat comes down when we win than when we lose, for reasons I don't fully understand. Part of it, no doubt, is that when we're stuck, we tend to push the betting ratio more and take other chances in order to win the money back. Perhaps we look more tense and thus draw more suspicion.

When things go poorly, it can be horrible. I can't count the times I've run all over town, trying to find a game. I'll go to one or two clubs, see familiar bosses, and split. Then it's off to another club—bad penetration. Finally you "get down" at a good game, play your heart out, and get killed.

You come home, asking yourself, "Why the hell do they bar us, anyway? We lose so damn often. I finally found a good game. I played the best I know how. Yet the seven thousand that was in my pocket four hours ago, isn't there anymore. Seven thousand dollars—70 one-hundred-dollar bills. Gone! A new car. Gone! One hundred cases of Scotch. Gone!

"If I went to work in a 'real' job, at least I'd have some money to show for working hard for a day. Why am I knocking my head against a wall, doing this?"

There's another aspect of blackjack playing that bothers me as much as any other:

In just about any other human endeavor, a person can get a good night's sleep, get up, ready to move mountains, and say, "Today I am really going to accomplish something."

Thus, a good chapter is written, a good business presentation is made, or an efficient computer sub-routine is programmed.

But when you play blackjack, you can have that same feeling, go out full of enthusiasm—and come back a loser.

Don't ever let anybody tell you that it's easy.

I took Neil to the Trop. I hadn't been there in six weeks. It was the first time I'd be in there with the wig. I confidently walked in, feeling protected by the wig and a new pair of sunglasses. I sat down at a $25 double-deck game.

Instantly, a boss I'd never seen before whispered to another boss. The second boss looked at me.

I had placed a $25 bet and was dealt a 20. I wanted to get out of there fast, before all the other bosses saw me in the wig. So I hit the 20, busted, and split to the distant four-deck pit. I peeked back at the main pit, from behind a pillar, to see if the "heat" may have been imagined.

No way. Three bosses were now looking in my direction.

I rapidly walked past the bar, beyond the poker room, and went into the gift shop.

I took off the wig and sunglasses and stuffed them in my pocket. I bought a baseball hat and put it on, sliding it down so my ears stuck out, Dumbo-the-Elephant style.

A security guard entered the gift shop. His eyes swept across the crowded store. He didn't recognize me. I walked right past him, out the exit. He didn't even blink.

As I walked out the door of the casino without the wig, another boss stared at me.

He knew me, either way.

Goodbye, Trop.

Rambo knew one of the casino hosts at the Dunes and arranged a credit line for $5,000. Allen took Rambo in the Dunes and called plays for him. Rambo was immediately accepted since, on his very first play, the host stood next to him as he was playing.

They comped Rambo to a suite, and for the next four days, Neil, Allen and I (wigged) called plays for him. Seven plays (and $6,200 in winnings) later, the dealers started shuffling on Rambo.

Rollie's friend, the one who knew so many bosses in town, called me. "One of the Dunes's bosses told me that you're lining up their credit players to play with your team. They're really pissed."

I was calling plays for Inga at the Imperial Palace. When I gave her end-of-session, she gave me a questioning look, to make sure she had read my signal correctly. At that very instant, a boss looked over at Inga, and then immediately looked at me.

Inga left, and I stayed. I heard the boss say to another boss, "I may be paranoid, but I think those two are together."

I played nickels by myself for an hour and a half to try to take the heat off.

The next time I was in the Imperial Palace on that shift, that same boss, upon seeing me, immediately looked to my left to see if there was a girl there.

He relaxed when he saw there wasn't. Neil was, though.

I sat down at third base of a Caesars' four-deck game (wig on). The dealer was a good-looking redhead, whom I'd played against without the wig. After 15 minutes, she turned to me and said in a friendly voice, "Hi. I almost didn't recognize you with the wig."

I almost explained, "Well, with the chemotherapy, I need either the baseball cap or the wig," But it didn't seem as if she thought a thing about the hairpiece.

I was wrong. When she went on break, she almost fell over herself running to the shift manager to tell him about her discovery. I quickly left, just as I overheard her say, "That guy at third base . . ."

The boss never saw my face. But it didn't do any good. The next day, the entire shift knew who I was.

A few years ago, we could cut corners and often get away with it. In 1986, this no longer seemed to be the case. Whenever we took a chance, or did something risky, it invariably came back to haunt us.

Playing as BP, Inga accepted a comp (for two) to the Riv's fabulous Delmonico restaurant. I snuck in fifteen minutes after Inga and joined her for the free dinner. I'd assumed that the bosses, who almost never are seen in gourmet rooms, would never be the wiser.

Somehow word got around (it wasn't the photo-domes—there weren't any in the restaurant). During dessert, a stream of bosses casually paraded by our table to have a good look.

In the long run, it would have been a lot cheaper to pay for dinner somewhere else.

Glynn and Neil had a completely cool play at the Hacienda on day shift. Glynn kept the play going, even though the swing shift bosses came on duty; he was chasing the $4,000 they were down.

Thirty minutes into the new shift, the boys got "one-half deck and shuffle" (out of two decks). The next day, Neil got shuffled up on by the day shift bosses, too.

We blew it again.

I was watching Glynn call plays for Rambo at the IP. Rambo won $4,650. When Rambo got up to leave, so, inexplicably, did Glynn.

I saw a boss follow Glynn to the cashier's cage, where he was standing in line behind Rambo. Glynn and Rambo were whispering to each other.

Ugh!

One of our team's top priorities obviously was to get more play. We had two rules which helped to promote this.

—Do not associate with each other IN ANY WAY in the casinos (comps or not).

—Do not play through shift changes (stuck or not).

We violated these rules and suffered the consequences.

We also drew heat because of other foolish errors.

I was playing at the Union Plaza and saw pictures on the pit stand. I stood up and glanced into the pit to see if the photos were of our team.

A boss who I hadn't noticed looked at me. Then he walked over to the pit and checked out the pictures.

I grabbed my chips and left the casino.

Smart move, Ken.

Caesars day and swing shifts had made me with the wig. So I went on graveyard, without the wig; for disguise, I used a baseball cap and glasses. I put the cap way back on my head; not only did my ears stick out, but it made me appear that I had a high forehead (usually my hair extends down to a few inches above the eyebrows).

The graveyard blackjack expert, Lefty, walked by my table with another boss. I heard snatches of their conversation:

". . . baseball player now. . . . no hair. . . . high forehead. . . . thinks he's got us fooled . . ."

They never said a word to me.

So I kept playing. To avoid "breaking it off," I never bet more than $200. (Two hundred dollars would be considered a big bet in just about any other casino in town. Caesars is used to—and caters to—high action; $500 players often get virtually no attention from the pit.)

At noon, the graveyard bosses disappeared, and were replaced with a new set of bosses.

This time, I purposely played through the shift change. The day shift manager saw me, did a double take, and said, "Kenny, what are you doing?"

"I've been playing all night. They let me go, as long as I stay under $200."

He thought a minute. Then he said, "You don't have any friends in here, do you?" (He was referring, of course, to BP's.)

I hadn't. "You've got my word. No."

He thought for a minute. "Go ahead. Enjoy yourself."

The following day, I played late day shift, purposely overlapped into swing. The ploy worked again; my $200 max bets were allowed on the third shift as well.

It was during this shift, a few days later, that I got some unexpected help from the pit. The bosses often watched me play; it was an opportunity for them to observe a known counter ply his trade, without trying to disguise his play with lots of cover betting.

Stuck over $5,000, the count suddenly soared. I put out $200, and said, "Boy. I wish I could bet two grand. It's sky high,"

The boss said, "I didn't hear anyone say how many hands you could play."

Message received. I put out two more $200 bets. That became my new maximum limit.

As I drew more and more heat in town, I played the Caesars game more frequently. Alas, all good things seem to come to an end. Within weeks, Caesars discontinued their attractive four-deck games.

After four hours at the Flamingo, a boss stood behind me in the aisle, never a good sign. When I turned around, another guy came walking up the aisle. "Hi, Kenny."

"What? My name's Thompson."

"Sure, I know. Tommy Thompson. Same name you used at the Sands. I'm with Griffin. Remember Richard Gonsalves? I took his place."

(Gonsalves was the Griffin guy who, years ago, would spot me wherever I went; for some reason, he could see through every disguise I'd ever worn.)

I said, "What the hell are you talking about?"

The boss was unsure. "There might be a mistake. Do you have ID?"

I became "indignant" and tried to put him on the defensive.

"I'm giving you my action, and you want me to show ID so I can play here? You got it backwards, buddy. I couldn't care less about this dump. If you don't want my action, I'll go back to Caesars. What's your Casino Manager's name, anyway?"

"Jerry Lewin."

I wrote it down and left in a huff.

The boss wasn't sure that the Griffin agent was right. But it didn't matter. Before long, the wig would be in the Mug Book.

I had been keeping a "Heat Table." Down one side was a listing of all the clubs. Across the top I wrote the names of our counters and BP's. In each space, I put an "X" (playable) or "O" (unplayable). When a club went from playable to unplayable, I drew an "O" around the "X".

As the days went by, the "O's" were beating out the "X's" by a huge margin.

It was time to go to Northern Nevada.

# 20

# We Finally Break a Bank

## No More Evidence

Some you win and some you lose. I just lost one. Judge Thompson dismissed my Motion for Additional Evidence. He agreed with the Attorney General's position that I should have introduced those facts at the Commission hearing.

I took another look at the statutes, and didn't agree with the judge. Who knows? This ruling might be a blessing in disguise. If the judge ruled incorrectly, and I lose the case, this decision could constitute a procedural error, which would be helpful in getting the Nevada Supreme Court to hear the case.

The new evidence may not really be necessary. As long as the Commission doesn't try to deny that the barrings took place, then, as Glen and Bill had said, it is "a matter of law" (i.e., the facts are not disputed; given agreed-upon facts, the only relevance is: What do the statues dictate?).

Interestingly, the judge, in his letter, added, "The opposition filed . . . by Intervenor Nevada Resort Association was filed without permission [sic] of this Court. Accordingly, the same is stricken."

That seems to imply that the judge is covering his tracks, making sure he's done everything by the book, procedurally. I suspect he's convinced I'm going to appeal if I lose.

I had dinner with two lawyer friends, who didn't exactly give me a vote of confidence. Both repeated the old adage, "A lawyer who represents himself has a fool for a client."

## "The Biggest Little City in the World"

There are plenty of casinos in Reno, but the town is a lot smaller than Vegas. I wondered what kind of inroads we'd be able to make here. The team set up camp in several hotel rooms.

Almost immediately we found that the two best games in town, by far, are at the Reno Hilton and the Cal-Neva.

—The Hilton game is as good as the best ones in Vegas—single deck, double on any two cards. The only negative rule is that, as in downtown Vegas, the house hits soft 17—a minor .2% sacrifice. The good news: the Hilton dealers deal further down than any single-deck game in Vegas. The penetration's unbelievable.

—The Cal-Neva used to be a horrible club, with standard Reno rules and no insurance. Now they've got double on 9 (as well as 10 and 11), surrender and insurance, for a minor .3% against the player.

Before long, it became obvious how best to play this game. With a −.2% off the top, and our huge bank, we can bet real large, and be dead-even with the house after seeing only one small card. If the card's a 2,3,4,6 or 7, we're about even; if the card's a 5, we have the edge.

I took Neil into the Hilton. Day shift was horrible. I signaled him $100 flat bets, and the pit watched the game like a hawk.

That evening, we played swing. A totally different environment. They loved Neil's action, and before long we were betting up to $500. The fact that we lost $7,000 may have accounted for our warm reception.

The following night, I again counted for Neil. I pretended that I'd met him at the tables and that we'd developed an instant friendship. We loudly asked each other where we were from and generally conducted ourselves like two recently befriended strangers.

The pit bought the ruse. One dealer started shuffling prematurely, making his table unplayable. After I lost two hands in a row, I stood up and loudly proclaimed to Neil, "This table's bad luck! Let's go somewhere else."

We both picked up our chips—like new-found buddies—and moved off to another table. The pit never blinked.

Neil went up about $5,000. Then the heat came down. A young collegiate-looking boss started watching our game intently. I suspected he was counting. Although I was laying out a conservative bet variation for Neil, with lots of camouflage, the boss seemed fascinated with Neil's betting strategy.

Another boss came up to him and said, "Time for your break."

The first boss, preoccupied, said, "Never mind. I'll stay for a while."

Now I've never *ever* seen a boss, due for break, who out of curiosity, interest in the game, or whatever reason stayed in the pit.

That did not augur well for us. I suspected the boss knew Neil was up to something and was trying to figure out what kind of subtle betting strategy we were using.

I signaled several crass "violation" bets to Neil.

They seemed to work; the boss relaxed and finally took his break.

But the point was, these pit guys were getting a lot smarter these days—and, in some cases, more dedicated.

Allen took Rambo to Harrah's. There, eight players—all huge men—were betting $100 chips at various tables. Allen suspected they were football coaches or trucking executives. Rambo sat down with the other high-rollers, and Allen gave him signals on-the-rail.

Rambo, who looks like one of those grunt-and-groan TV wrestlers, blended in perfectly with the hefty high-rollers. He drew minimal attention, but Allen had to keep giving him "change tables," because of the spotty penetration.

Rambo won $6,600 and was comped to a suite.

## The Five Reasons Why Counters Fail—And How to Avoid Them

I flew back to San Francisco to work on the lawsuit. The minute I walked in the door, the phone rang. It was from Chuck, a commodities exchange trader in Chicago, who'd read my previous book. He had some questions. I'm going to report our conversation verbatim, because Chuck's questions were so typical of the ones I get every day and reflected such common misconceptions about playing blackjack.

"Ken, I'm thinking about making a living playing blackjack. What are my chances of success?"

"I hate to tell you this, but they're really low."

"Is it unrealistic to expect a daily income from playing blackjack?"

"It's out of the question. The swings are extreme. Don't even think about a daily income. To give you an idea, even assuming that you studied hard, became real good, and began to play full-time, it's a 1-out-of-5 shot that after a month of playing you'd be in the hole. So not only can't you be sure of a daily income, you can't even plan on a monthly income.

"That's why I form teams. Instead of playing alone, getting in eight hours a day, we can get in 40 hours a day, with four teammates; that's the equivalent of a solitary player playing for a week. Thus we get into the long run quicker and keep the fluctuations down, which is the biggest ulcer-creating factor in blackjack."

Chuck asked, "Why do you say my chances of success are low?"

"It takes far too much discipline for the average person."

Chuck said, "If I have anything, it's discipline. I like hard work."

"Well, let me just tell you this. There are five basic reasons why counters or teams fail:

"First, improper or inadequate training. You can overcome this by setting up and following strict training guidelines.

"Second, inadequate bankroll viz-á-viz betting levels. You've got to keep your bet size low enough so you can withstand the fluctuations, which, as I said, are huge.

"Third, playing unprofitable games. You've got to make sure you get good penetration—35 cards in a single-deck game, 1½ decks in a double-deck game, over three out of four decks, and five out of six decks.

"Four, inadequate self-discipline. You've got to play only when rested and adhere strictly to your betting schedule and general game plan—and also make sure all team members are honest.

"Five, getting barred. You've got to make counter measures to make sure your playing life is maximized, such as using a BP, putting on a good act in the casino, and avoiding overplaying a given casino so you eventually get thrown out."

Chuck asked again, "What are my chances of making a living from blackjack?"

"I'm sorry to have to say this, but the chances are real high that the average counter or team organizer, even knowing these five pitfalls, will still fail. Teams usually fall apart when they're losing. To get even, teammates overbet their bankrolls, cut corners, play sloppily, and take chances. It's real tough."

## Now It's Up to the Judge

In my opening brief, I'd argued "the law," that is, made what I felt was a strong case that the exclusion of skilled players by Nevada casinos was contrary to Nevada law (the statutes, common law, and case precedent).

Then I received the Attorney General's reply brief, which claimed that much of my argument was irrelevant because I'd asked for a rule change. Their point: the courts have no business overruling the Commission, a quasi-legislative body which makes regulations. For the courts to get into this area violates the separation of powers doctrines of the State of Nevada, which delineates the respective authority of the legislative, executive and judicial branches of the state.

They had a point, and cited several Nevada cases which seemed to nail down their position.

Of course, the only reason I'd requested a rule change in the first place was because of the suggestion of the Chairman of the Gaming Control Board. I had figured I'd better go along with him (I suspected that the Chairman had the power to arbitrarily throw out my request, if he wanted) and that it was better to get my foot in the door and see what happens. At the time, in my naiveté, I had no idea what the implications of going for a rule change were, as opposed to just requesting a hearing.

But the Attorney General also claimed that the Chairman of the Control Board could not speak for the Commission.

I called Bill and said, "What do I do now?"

Bill said, "Estop." Bill went on to explain the principle of "estoppel," which basically said that if Party A is led by Party B into an act that is detrimental to his position, then Party A is entitled to relief.

It was time for two days in the law library researching "estoppel," and another two days preparing the brief. It was fun, challenging, and once again I felt optimistic about our position.

I centered the Reply Brief around two basic points:

1. I had been induced into seeking a rule change, which was detrimental to me. Because of this, I was entitled to whatever relief I would have been entitled to, had I not so been led.

2. The Chairman of the Board is the top full-time gaming regulator in the State, and he wrote me on official Nevada letterhead, with the name of the governor and the Official Seal of the State of Nevada imprinted thereon. Thus, he was authorized to act for the state, and I reacted accordingly.

But another shoe had yet to drop—the reply brief from the Nevada Resort Association.

Finally the NRA brief came through. Their basic point was that I have no right, by Nevada law, to re-litigate this issue. I'd filed suits against several Nevada casinos in the late 70's. The suits had been dismissed and were now coming back to haunt me.

I dug up some legal arguments that said, basically, that the matters involved in the earlier Nevada lawsuits were far from the subjects now at issue. Thus the current case was a litigation of new factors. I can't say I felt these arguments were overwhelmingly convincing.

At any rate, the battle lines were now drawn. It was time to wait for the oral argument in court. Then it would all be up to "De Judge."

## The Horseshoe Offers to Cough Up

Allen Brown phoned.

"Ken, the Horseshoe offered to settle with us. Les [Combs, the lawyer] wants to make a counter-offer. I'll tell you what the figures are. But first, I'd like to ask you what you think the cases are worth."

"Any permanent damage?"

"No. But I had 10 broken ribs and Barry had three. You also know about the internal contusions—and I *did* almost die."

I said, "Well, I do know that Jonathan Unger got $100,000, and he wasn't hurt as bad as you. Yet who knows what a jury and judge will do in Vegas?"

Allen interjected, "Well, you were probably hurt as bad as anyone at the Mapes."

"My settlement is no indication because my lawyer for some reason kept pushing me to settle real low. Also at the time I was involved in lots more important things, and didn't bother really pursuing the lawsuit aggressively."

Allen said, "We can definitely prove in court that they did it. The Vegas police have been real cooperative."

"What were your medical costs?"

"Mine were thirty thou, mostly insured. Barry's were less. They also took $5,000 in chips away from us in the backroom."

"I assume Les gets a third?"

"Yes."

I said, "Well, I hesitate to take a guess. It all depends on what a jury—and the judge—may do, and that's sheer speculation. You know, judge's do reduce awards, like in the Carol Burnett-*National Enquirer* case and the Lee Marvin-Mitchelson palimony suit. Did this judge ever reduce a jury award before?"

"I don't know. I'll ask Les."

"Have you researched past settlements in Nevada?"

"Yeah. As far as we can determine, the top settlement has been 100 thou—but we were hurt a lot worse."

"Well, this is a gross guess. But if it were me, I'd probably go for maybe double what Jonathan got—around 200 to 250 thousand."

"The Horseshoe offered me $150,000 and Barry $75,000. Les wants to counter-offer for $400,000 and $200,000. He says if we ask for lots more, the judge may be prejudiced against us, thinking we're really greedy."

After we hung up, I made a few calculations. If they were to roughly split the difference of $300,000 for Allen, Les would get $100,000, and Allen, after the medical bills he paid and the $5,000 in chips, would clear about $185,000.

That's a lot of money. But would you undergo 10 broken ribs, contusions of the lung, kidney, spleen and kidney, and risk death for $185,000? (On that day, lots of Americans, including me, were thinking about the risk of death, because that was the very day that the NASA Space Shuttle exploded, killing the seven brave souls on board.)

## The Barrings Continue

A counter from Vegas called with an urgent message.

"Ken, I just got dragged across the floor at the Flamingo. Griffin spotted me. I got 'back-roomed.' I was playing nickels—for about an hour—and several security guards grabbed me, dragged me into a back room, and hassled me. They held me up, against my will, so they could take my picture. My thigh and arms are swollen and have contusions.

"When the cops came, they were on my side. One of 'em said, 'Sue the bastards for felony false imprisonment.'

"I called a lawyer, and that's what I'm doing."

After I hung up, I wondered when, if ever, this absurd behavior would end. More than ever I hoped Judge Thompson, or a higher judge, would put an end to these absurdities. The barrings, hasslings, and back-roomings seem to go on interminably. This couldn't be the level of justice in America in the '80s—even if it was Nevada.

## Creamed In Court

We finally got to the Las Vegas District Court on February 12, 1986. To say that I was nervous was an understatement. I'd never presented oral argument in front of a judge before.

I talked from a flip chart presentation, which summarized the key points—namely, that the Court could overturn the Commission for any of nine reasons:

—four key points of law were ignored by the Commission,
—three procedural violations were committed,
—the Commission's ruling was "arbitrary," and
—the Commission hadn't sufficiently considered the evidence.

If I was able to prove *any* of the nine points, the Court, by law, must overturn the Commission.

Then the Deputy Attorney General gave his oral argument, stressing that I had asked for a regulation change, and that the court did not have jurisdiction to order a rule change, which is a legislative, not a judicial, function (again, the suggestion to me by the Gaming

Control Board Chairman was coming back to haunt me).

The lawyer for the Nevada Resort Association then argued that New Jersey rulings do not apply to Nevada, for various reasons.

I was permitted to make a rebuttal argument and argued "estoppel," pointing out that I was led by the opposition to ask for a rule change, but merely wanted a hearing and the right to play blackjack. Thus I should be entitled to the relief I would have received had I not been so misled. I felt both comfortable and confident during the rebuttal presentation.

To my astonishment, immediately after I sat down, Judge Thompson, without having asked even a single question, commented briefly that he didn't think that his court had jurisdiction. I was stunned when he ended with a simple "Petition denied."

## Computers and Jail

It was just a matter of time. A fellow named Tom Hyland—he used to run conventional blackjack teams in New Jersey and Nevada—was caught using a blackjack computer in Nassau.

Hyland had about $100,000 in money and chips, which the Bahamians confiscated. They threw him into a dingy, dark jail cell overnight.

There's no hard and fast law about computers in the Bahamas. But the Bahamian officials hastily judged Hyland guilty. They also circulated his picture among casinos around the world.

## We Finally Break a Bank

Rambo, with Glynn and Allen, beat Harrah's for $17,500, putting our overall team win at just over $125,000. Although our net win was below $125,000 after expenses, we were all psychologically ready to break the bank.

We converged on Rambo's suite—a palatial mega-suite on the top floor of Harrah's, where their Headliners stayed. The team gathered in an opulent master bedroom. On the bed was nearly a quarter of a million dollars in cash and chips.

We'd won a lot of money—but it reflected many months of playing and enormous expenses, and there were lots of players to split up the boodle.

We ordered room service—a half dozen bottles of booze and wine; for security purposes we didn't order dinners. For 5½ hours, I made a complex series of calculations, from dozens of worksheets we'd kept over the previous months, tallying the number of hours played by each counter, each BP, the win and loss for each counter, the amount of cash physically put in by each investor, and the expenses paid by each team member. Then we tried to reconcile our cash win with our win on paper. We finally balanced to within $2,600 (on the short side, as it always seems to be) and considered ourselves lucky (at one point, we thought we were short $16,700). Finally the books balanced and we had calculated how much everyone would receive.

It was strange. After breaking banks in the past, the talk almost immediately turned to the formation of the next bank. This didn't come close to happening here. The "trip" was so long, so tough and arduous, the training so intense, and the fluctuations so extreme, that not a single team member was anxious to start another trip. Most of us wanted to savor the win, the nice thick stacks of hundred-dollar bills, the ensuing vacation—and forget about fluctuations, barrings, "stiffs," and cover betting.

We planned to take at least two months off. Then we would meet in San Francisco to launch our next effort. Although no one wanted to commit to a precise date, we did make some general plans: We would play periodically, not intensely, at the most attractive games in Nevada; we wouldn't bother yet with New Jersey or abroad. While they were fresh in our minds, we made a list of the best games in Nevada, which were:

Vegas Single Deck: Landmark, Circus, Mint.

Vegas Double Deck, excellent penetration: Trop, Sands, IP, Riviera, Sundance, Lady Luck.

Vegas Double Deck, fair penetration, depending upon the dealer and shift: Dunes, Flamingo, Hacienda.

Vegas Four Deck: Sands, El Rancho, Bourbon Street.

Alas, Caesars was now six deck, and not worth playing.

Reno Single Deck, excellent rules: Hilton.

Reno Single Deck, average rules but good penetration (usually): Harrah's, Harold's Club.

Lake Tahoe: Harrah's, Harvey's, High Sierra.

Everyone had plans for a well-deserved rest.

Rambo said, "I'm going to Club Med and may not come back for a month." Neil planned to fly back east to visit his family.

Allen added, "Man, I'm going to Newport and romp on the beaches with the bikini ladies."

Glynn: "I won the down payment on a lot I've been looking at in Concord. Now I can close the deal."

Inga and I would return to the Bay Area. Inga would take care of our new pug puppy. I'd do some writing and work on the lawsuit.

## Off to the Supreme Court

It took five weeks' work to get all the papers, pleadings, bonds, fees, and other minutiae in proper order for my appeal to the Supreme Court of Nevada. Finally on May 2, 1986, everything was submitted.

After the debacle in District Court, I was far less confident about the objectivity of the court system in Nevada. The fact that Nevada Supreme Court justices are elected, and thus subject to pressure from campaign contributions, didn't seem to augur well for our side.

I continue to be astonished that Nevada casinos offer a game of skill to the general public, and then allow the unskillful, degenerate, and compulsive gamblers to play, and arbitrarily throw out, detain, photograph, and even beat up patrons who they suspect are skillful.

If I lose at the state Supreme Court level, I'll try to bring the case before the U.S. Supreme Court. But that's a real long shot. The U.S. Supreme Court receives thousands of requests for hearings each year, and it hears just over 100 cases annually. The odds are at least 100-to-1 against you. And one must wonder just how significant the court would view the rather narrow issue of casino exclusion of blackjack players.

Even if turned down by the highest court, I plan to start the process over again by getting barred and then filing with federal court in Nevada. I refuse to give up on this issue, even if it takes another 10 years.

## I Finally Get to Play

I've wanted to play jazz piano ever since I was in college. I recall, when at Harvard Business School, that I'd walk to the dining hall for lunch, sit down at the Steinway to avoid waiting in line for lunch, and, totally absorbed, continue to play until my classmates came back for dinner at 5:00 P.M.

Well, after over 20 years, I've finally formed a jazz trio, called "GarnerJazz" (after the late Erroll Garner), with nationally-known bassist Herbie Lewis, who's played with Sarah Vaughn, Les McCann, and a number of other well-known jazz artists.

"GarnerJazz" is now the center of my life; every day I look forward to the rehearsals, "gigs," and jam sessions around the Bay Area.

And what's really nice is that they don't throw me out for playing too well.

# Appendix

## The Rules of the Game

### OBJECT OF THE GAME

To obtain a total higher than that of the dealer, but not greater than 21.

### BASIC RULES

Before any cards are dealt, the players place their bets.

The dealer deals cards from his left to his right, one by one. The players and the dealer get two cards.

The players' cards may be dealt either face up or face down, depending upon the rules of the house. The dealer receives one card face up, called the upcard, and one card face down, the hole-card.

The 2 through 10 cards are worth their face denomination. Jacks, queens, and kings are worth 10 points. The ace is counted as either 1 or 11.

A hand that has an ace that can be counted as 11 without the total of the hand exceeding 21 is called a "soft" hand. All other hands are called "hard" hands.

Casinos typically use from one to eight decks of cards. Many casinos in Reno and Lake Tahoe use one deck. Las Vegas casinos deal one-, two-, four-, six-, seven-, and eight-deck games. Atlantic City casinos usually provide six- and eight-deck games.

### "BLACKJACK"

If the first two cards received by either a player or the dealer are a 10-valued card and an ace, that hand is called a "blackjack."

If the player has a blackjack, he receives one and one-half times his original bet. If the dealer has a blackjack, all players who do not have a blackjack lose. If the player and dealer both have blackjacks, the hand is tied.

### HITTING

The player may take additional cards (or "hit"), if he chooses, as long as his hand does not total more than hard 21.

The player signals for a hit by:

—scratching the table-top with his finger or fingers (in games where the cards are dealt face up).

—scratching the table-top with his two cards (in games where the cards are dealt face down).

### STANDING

The player may refuse to draw additional cards (or "stand"). The player stands by:

—moving his fingers or hand in a lateral motion (in games where the cards are dealt face up).

—sliding his cards face-down under his bet (in games where the cards are dealt face down).

### BUSTING

If the player's hand exceeds a total of hard 21, he has "busted" and loses the hand.

If the dealer busts, all players who have not busted win the hand.

### DEALER DRAWING

The dealer must hit until he has a total of 17. In some casinos, notably those in downtown Las Vegas, Reno and Lake Tahoe, the dealer must hit soft 17.

## PUSH

If the dealer and the player have the same total (under 21), the hand is considered a tie (or "push"), and no money exchange takes place.

## DOUBLING-DOWN

After receiving his first two cards, the player may double the amount of his bet and draw one more card only.

Some casinos restrict the totals on which players may double down. (For example, in Reno and Lake Tahoe, most casinos allow the player to double down only on hands totalling 10 and 11.)

Many casinos allow the player to "double for less" than the amount of the original bet.

## SPLITTING PAIRS

If the player receives two cards of identical value he may "split" them into two hands, and put out an amount equal to his original bet.

The player plays each hand as a separate hand. If the player receives another card identical to the first two, as the first card on one of the split cards, he may split the pair again ("resplit"). Some casinos allow splitting and re-splitting three times on a single original hand; some casinos allow only two splits; some allow an indefinite number of splits.

## DOUBLING-DOWN ON SPLIT PAIRS

Some casinos allow the player to double down after he has split a pair. For example, assume the player had a pair of 9's and split them, putting out another bet. Assume the player drew a 2 on the first nine. If he chooses, the player can double down on this hand, putting out another amount equal to his original bet.

Most casinos in Nevada do not allow this practice. As of this writing, all Atlantic City casinos, in accordance with New Jersey Commission regulations, permit players to double down on split pairs.

SURRENDER

Some casinos allow the player, after he has seen his first two cards, to throw in his hand and forfeit half of his original bet. However, the player may not surrender if the dealer has a blackjack.

INSURANCE

If the dealer has an ace upcard, the player is allowed to bet an amount equal to half his original bet, wagering that the dealer has a blackjack. If the dealer has blackjack, the player is paid 2 for 1 on this side bet.

## Basic Strategy

The computers of many blackjack experts have developed an identical set of rules, called Basic Strategy, which tell us the best way to play blackjack hands.

Basic Strategy assumes the player is not a counter. The counting player, on occasion, will make plays contrary to Basic Strategy because he is aware of variations in the content of the remaining cards to be dealt.

Basic Strategy varies slightly, depending on whether a single deck or multiple decks are being used. Basic Strategy also varies depending upon the player options permitted by the house, and whether the dealer hits or stands on soft 17.

HARD HITTING:

Most of the hands played by the player are covered by three simple rules which NEVER CHANGE. These rules cover hard hitting and standing, and are as follows:

1. If the dealer has a 2 or 3 upcard, hit until you reach a total of hard 13.

2. If the dealer has a 4, 5 or 6 upcard, hit until you reach a total of hard 12.

3. If the dealer has a 7 or 8 upcard, hit until you reach a total of hard 17.

SOFT HITTING:

There are only two rules for soft hands:

4. If the dealer has a 9 or 10 upcard, hit until you reach a total of soft 19.*

5. If the dealer has anything else, hit until you reach a total of soft 18.

INSURANCE:

Never take insurance.

These six simple rules, which you can learn in 10 minutes, cover more than 70% of the hands you will play!

## Reno or Lake Tahoe

If you're playing in Reno or Lake Tahoe, there are only nine more rules that need to be learned.

DOUBLING DOWN:

| *If Your Hand Totals:* | *Double Down If the Dealer Upcard Is:* |
|---|---|
| 11 | Any Card |
| 10 | 2 through 9 |

SPLITTING PAIRS:

| *If Your Hand is:* | *Split If the Dealer Upcard Is:* |
|---|---|
| Ace, Ace | Any Card |
| 9,9 | 2 through 9, but not 7 |
| 8,8 | Any Card |
| 7,7 | 2 through 7 |
| 6,6 | 2 through 6 |
| 3,3 | 4 through 7 |
| 2,2 | 3 through 7 |

The rules are unfavorable in Reno or Lake Tahoe, because of the restriction on doubling-down and because the house hits soft 17.

*One refinement that is not critical: if the dealer hits soft 17, hit A,7 (and other soft 18's) versus an ace.

Therefore, only play single deck games in those locations. The great majority of games in Northern Nevada are single deck.

## Las Vegas

When playing in Vegas, there are a few more rules to learn, which cover additional doubling-down options.

DOUBLING-DOWN:

| *If Your Hand Totals:* | *Double Down If the Dealer Upcard Is:* |
|---|---|
| 11 | Any Card |
| 10 | 2 through 9 |
| 9 | 2 through 6 |
| A,8 | 6 |
| A,7 A,6 | 3 through 6 |
| A,5 A,4 / A,3 A2 | 4 through 6 |

With these rules, playing single deck in Las Vegas, you are now dead even with the house!

MULTIPLE DECK GAMES:

If you're playing multiple deck games in Las Vegas, make the following adjustments to the above rules:

| *Your Hand* | *Action* |
|---|---|
| 11 | Double with dealer's 2 through 10 |
| 9 | Double with dealer's 3 through 6 |
| A,8 | Never double; always stand |
| A,6 | Double with dealer's 3 through 6 |
| A,3 | Double with dealer's 5 and 6 |
| A,2 | Double with dealer's 5 and 6 |
| 6,6 | Split with dealer's 3 through 6 |
| 2,2 | Split with dealer's 4 through 7 |

**Atlantic City**

The Atlantic City strategy is the same for all casinos, since the blackjack rules are specifically defined by the New Jersey Casino Control Commission.

—The hard and soft standing rules are identical to those described above.

—The doubling-down and splitting rules are as follows:

| *Your Hand* | *Action* |
|---|---|
| 11 | Double with dealer's 2 through 10 |
| 10 | Double with dealer's 2 through 9 |
| 9 | Double with dealer's 3 through 6 |
| | |
| A,8 | Never double; always stand |
| A,7 A,6 | Double with dealer's 3 through 6 |
| A,5 A,4 | Double with dealer's 4 through 6 |
| A,3 A,2 | Double with dealer's 5 through 6 |
| | |
| Ace, Ace | Always Split |
| 9,9 | 2 through 9, but not 7 |
| 8,8 | Always Split |
| 7,7 | 2 through 7 |
| 6,6 | 2 through 6 |
| 4,4 | 5 and 6 |
| 3,3 2,2 | 2 through 7 |

**Card-Counting**

Card-counters are able to get an edge over the house because they keep track of the types of cards played. When a sufficiently high proportion of 10's and aces are in the deck(s), the player has an edge over the house. When a high proportion of low cards remain in the deck(s), the house has a greater advantage over the player.

The card-counter does not really count cards. He keeps track of the types of cards that are played, and knows when the deck(s) favors the player and when it favors the house.

When the deck(s) favors the player, he puts out large bets. When the deck(s) favor the house, the counter bets small. The weighted average of these bets, gives the counter an edge over the house.

The card-counter also varies his play, depending upon the content of the deck. When the deck is rich in 10's, for example, he may split 10's versus a dealer's 6, ordinarily a foolish play. If the deck is full of low cards, he might hit 14 versus a 4, usually an unwise play.

Responsible counting systems assign plus "+" values to low cards and minus "−" values to aces and high cards. Using such a system, the counter keeps a running count of the cards played.

Although there are dozens of texts available on card-counting, I would recommend four books: two that teach card-counting, simply and clearly, and two that give interesting historical perspectives on the game.

The player interested in learning how to card-count would be well advised to read:

1 Arnold Snyder's book, *Blackbelt in Blackjack*, $12.95, RGE Publishing, 2000 Center Street, #1067, Berkeley, CA 94704.

2. *Million Dollar Blackjack*, by Ken Uston, $14.95, at local bookstores.

3. Arnold Snyder's *Quarterly Blackjack Forum* (complimentary sample copy available from address above).

Also, learn either the Uston SS Count* or Arnold Snyder's Zen Count.

Recent studies by Snyder and by blackjack expert Stanford Wong have revealed that counts requiring ace adjustment, such as the Revere 14 Count, the Uston Advanced Point Count, and Hi Opt I or II, are simply not worth the effort. The player will lose more from errors and fatigue than he will gain from attempting to use such complicated systems.

If you're interested in the historical development of winning at the game of blackjack, I'd recommend two additional books:

Edward O. Thorp's *Beat The Dealer, A Winning Strategy For The Game Of Twenty-One*. New York: Random House, 1966 (original version: 1962).

Lawrence Revere's *Playing Blackjack As A Business*. Secaucus, N.J.: Lyle Stuart, 1971 (revised versions: 1973, 1975, 1977, 1979).

*Write Uston Institute of Blackjack, 2410 Taylor Street, #1201, San Francisco, CA 94133, for information.